Divorce

Other Books in the Social Issues Firsthand Series:

Abortion
Adoption
Capital Punishment
Child Abuse
Death and Dying
Drug Abuse
The Environment
Family Violence
Gambling
Hate Crimes
Homosexuality
Immigration
Interracial Relationships
Poverty
Prisons
Religion
Suicide
Terrorism
Violence

Divorce

Laurie Willis, Book Editor

GREENHAVEN PRESS

An imprint of Thomson Gale, a part of The Thomson Corporation

Detroit • New York • San Francisco • New Haven, Conn. • Waterville, Maine • London

Christine Nasso, *Publisher*
Elizabeth Des Chenes, *Managing Editor*

For more information, contact:
Greenhaven Press
27500 Drake Rd.
Farmington Hills, MI 48331-3535
Or you can visit our Internet site at http://www.gale.com

Articles in Greenhaven Press anthologies are often edited for length to meet page requirements. In addition, original titles of these works are changed to clearly present the main thesis and to explicitly indicate the author's opinion. Every effort is made to ensure that Greenhaven Press accurately reflects the original intent of the authors. Every effort has been made to trace the owners of copyrighted material.

Cover photograph reproduced by permission of photos.com.

ISBN-13: 978-0-7377-3837-7 (hardcover)
ISBN-10: 0-7377-3837-5 (hardcover)

Library of Congress Control Number: 2007934716

Contents

Chapter 3: Moving On

Chapter 4: The Children's Point of View

Foreword

Social issues are often viewed in abstract terms. Pressing challenges such as poverty, homelessness, and addiction are viewed as problems to be defined and solved. Politicians, social scientists, and other experts engage in debates about the extent of the problems, their causes, and how best to remedy them. Often overlooked in these discussions is the human dimension of the issue. Behind every policy debate over poverty, homelessness, and substance abuse, for example, are real people struggling to make ends meet, to survive life on the streets, and to overcome addiction to drugs and alcohol. Their stories are ubiquitous and compelling. They are the stories of everyday people—perhaps your own family members or friends—and yet they rarely influence the debates taking place in state capitols, the national Congress, or the courts.

The disparity between the public debate and private experience of social issues is well illustrated by looking at the topic of poverty. Each year the U.S. Census Bureau establishes a poverty threshold. A household with an income below the threshold is defined as poor, while a household with an income above the threshold is considered able to live on a basic subsistence level. For example, in 2003 a family of two was considered poor if its income was less than $12,015; a family of four was defined as poor if its income was less than $18,810. Based on this system, the bureau estimates that 35.9 million Americans (12.5 percent of the population) lived below the poverty line in 2003, including 12.9 million children below the age of eighteen.

Commentators disagree about what these statistics mean. Social activists insist that the huge number of officially poor Americans translates into human suffering. Even many families that have incomes above the threshold, they maintain, are likely to be struggling to get by. Other commentators insist that the statistics exaggerate the problem of poverty in the United States. Compared to people in developing countries, they point out, most so-called poor families have a high quality of life. As stated by journalist Fidelis Iyebote, "Cars are owned by 70 percent of 'poor' households. . . . Color televisions belong to 97 percent of the 'poor' [and] videocassette recorders belong to nearly 75 percent. . . . Sixty-four percent have microwave ovens, half own a stereo system, and over a quarter possess an automatic dishwasher."

However, this debate over the poverty threshold and what it means is likely irrelevant to a person living in poverty. Simply put, poor people do not need the government to tell them whether they are poor. They can see it in the stack of bills they cannot pay. They are aware of it when they are forced to choose between paying rent or buying food for their children. They become painfully conscious of it when they lose their homes and are forced to live in their cars or on the streets. Indeed, the written stories of poor people define the meaning of poverty more vividly than a government bureaucracy could ever hope to. Narratives composed by the poor describe losing jobs due to injury or mental illness, depict horrific tales of childhood abuse and spousal violence, recount the loss of friends and family members. They evoke the slipping away of social supports and government assistance, the descent into substance abuse and addiction, the harsh realities of life on the streets. These are the perspectives on poverty that are too often omitted from discussions over the extent of the problem and how to solve it.

Greenhaven Press's Social Issues Firsthand series provides a forum for the often-overlooked human perspectives on society's most divisive topics of debate. Each volume focuses on one social issue and presents a collection of ten to sixteen narratives by those who have had personal involvement with the topic. Extra care has been taken to include a diverse range of perspectives. For example, in the volume on adoption, readers will find the stories of birth parents who have made an adoption plan, adoptive parents, and adoptees themselves. After exposure to these varied points of view, the reader will have a clearer understanding that adoption is an intense, emotional experience full of joyous highs and painful lows for all concerned.

The debate surrounding embryonic stem cell research illustrates the moral and ethical pressure that the public brings to bear on the scientific community. However, while nonexperts often criticize scientists for not considering the potential negative impact of their work, ironically the public's reaction against such discoveries can produce harmful results as well. For example, although the outcry against embryonic stem cell research in the United States has resulted in fewer embryos being destroyed, those with Parkinson's, such as actor Michael J. Fox, have argued that prohibiting the development of new stem cell lines ultimately will prevent a timely cure for the disease that is killing Fox and thousands of others.

Each book in the series contains several features that enhance its usefulness, including an in-depth introduction, an annotated table of contents, bibliographies for further research, a list of organizations to contact, and a thorough index. These elements—combined with the poignant voices of people touched by tragedy and triumph—make the Social Issues Firsthand series a valuable resource for research on today's topics of political discussion.

Introduction

Acceptable reasons for divorce have historically reflected the culture of both time and place. Although a marriage license is a legal contract in many cultures, the social and religious norms of the prevailing culture generally affect the laws surrounding divorce.

Divorce Forbidden

In predominantly Christian countries, marriage and divorce have long been under the jurisdiction of the church. The Roman Catholic Church treats marriage as sacred. From the Middle Ages until the nineteenth century, the Church, and therefore many Catholic countries, did not permit divorce at all, instead requiring an annulment, which is a formal religious declaration that the marriage never existed. This stance has relaxed over time. In many Catholic cultures, members are able to obtain a civil divorce without being barred from the church. However, remarriage after divorce still usually requires an annulment to receive the church's blessing. In some largely Catholic countries such as Chile, there are no divorce laws even today. Chileans wishing to divorce need to go through a complicated annulment process under the pretext that there was an error made during the original marriage ceremony. Brazilians received the right to divorce legally only in 1977.

Divorce Easier for Men

Divorce laws and customs in many societies favor men over women. Often, women have been forbidden to initiate a divorce for any reason, whereas men have been allowed to divorce for very specific reasons, or sometimes for no reason at all. In ancient Rome, only men were permitted to divorce, and they could only do so if their wife was guilty of adultery, poisoning her children, or counterfeiting a key. In ancient Israel, a man could give his wife a bill of divorce, but she had no right to divorce him. In modern Israel divorce is permitted, but a man still has the right to prevent his former wife from remarrying. A divorced woman in Malawi must go back to her family, and the man retains all of the couples' property. Chinese women did not have the right to initiate a divorce until 1949.

In some Islamic cultures, a man needs only to say "I divorce you" three times to terminate a marriage. The wife must wait three months before she is free to remarry. In Islamic law, one type of divorce, a *khul'*, can be initiated by a woman if she repays her dowry or gives her husband some other form of compensation. In some forms of Islam, this is a woman's only option. In others, she may seek divorce because of nonsupport, abandonment, or "injury" (which is sometimes defined loosely to mean emotional as well as physical injury).

Divorce Allowed for Specific Reasons

Some cultures allow divorce but only for very specific reasons. In India, there are five main grounds for divorce: adultery, desertion, cruelty, impotence, and chronic disease. In the United States, grounds for divorce have always been regulated by each individual state, rather than by the federal government, and each state's laws are slightly different. Until very recently in the United States, a person filing for divorce needed to prove that their spouse did something that caused the need for divorce. Some commonly accepted causes have been adultery, bigamy, cruelty, desertion, and mental illness. During the last four decades in the United States, the need to prove one of these conditions has gradually eroded.

Relaxed Divorce Laws

There are many cultures today where divorce is far less complicated. Countries as widely spread as Nigeria, Thailand, and Australia have similar customs, where the couple is merely expected to divide their property and provide for the care of their children.

In the United States, the Family Law Act of California in 1969 was the first legislation permitting what is known as "no fault" divorce, in which a couple can simply decide to divorce without either partner being legally at fault. "Irreconcilable differences" became a recognized reason for divorce. By 1985, all fifty states had similar laws.

Social Pressures Against Divorce

In addition to determining the ability to obtain a divorce, social customs have also influenced the frequency of divorce. Until recently, divorce was frowned upon in the United States. Divorced women, in particular, were considered a threat, as people were concerned that a divorcée might steal another woman's husband. Economically, divorced and single women have not always been able to find employment and have frequently been paid lower wages than men. Many couples stayed together "for the sake of the children," since single mothers or fathers were not common and did not fit into society's picture of what "family" should be. Therefore, even a woman with a valid reason for divorce—for example, physical abuse to herself or her children—would hesitate to file for divorce because of the social pressures put on her.

Many Factors

As we have seen, whether or not a couple gets divorced is not a clear-cut matter. Reasons change with respect to time, place, legal requirements, social pressures, and practical factors.

Social Issues Firsthand: Divorce presents personal narratives about divorce from a number of perspectives, from the initial breakup to the process of finalizing the divorce through legal and religious channels, and then to the adventure of moving on and beginning a new life. In the final chapter, children whose parents have divorced present stories from their point of view.

CHAPTER 1

Breaking Up

Telling Him It's Over

Wendy Swallow

When Wendy Swallow was looking for books to help her through the difficult process of getting a divorce, she was surprised at how few books she found that were written in the style of a memoir, from personal experience. So, she decided to write a book about her own divorce.

In this excerpt, she has made the difficult decision to file for divorce because she felt that she and her children were drowning beneath her husband's fearful and negative attitudes. She describes telling him of her decision, his reaction, and the subsequent couples' counseling that they attended. The counseling helped her to confirm that they were very different people and she was ready to proceed with the divorce.

Ron [my husband] was out on the porch, reading. I went out and closed the door behind me.

"We need to talk." He put his book down and nodded, as if he had been expecting it. "I can't, I can't go on like this," I stumbled. "I think we need to split up."

He looked at me with such deep seriousness I couldn't tell what he was thinking. I had begged him several months earlier to go with me for marital counseling, but he had said at the time that he feared counseling would lead inevitably to splitting up. Now, though, he seemed to sense my desperation. "Okay," he said. "Let's talk this out."

Talking It Out

Over the next hour, I told Ron in unvarnished terms what was in my head and heart. I told him I felt like an intruder in my own house, that I was so clearly irritating to him that I was

Wendy Swallow, *Breaking Apart: A Memoir of Divorce*. New York: Hyperion, 2001.

walking on eggshells, fearful all the time that I would trigger his anger. He admitted I often bothered him—by the way I talked, by my continued allegiance to my family, by choices I made for the kids, by what he saw as certain lapses of good judgment. Instead of defending myself, as I had in the past, I simply responded that my problems didn't justify the level of anger and distrust in our marriage and that I wanted the boys to grow up with something different. We didn't talk about the lost intimacy between us, the lack of love in the house, but it was there, the monster crouched between us. The shadows of the boys hovered about us as well.

"I have the number of a divorce lawyer," I said. "I'm going to call him in the morning."

Ron flinched. "Please don't do that," he said. "I realize you're serious. I'm ready to go to marriage counseling if you want."

Trying Counseling

Counseling. A few months earlier I would have welcomed that, but now I could feel my momentum begin to drain from me. Counseling would throw me back into the marriage, back into the cycle of promises and effort, back into the marriage bed. I didn't know if I could do it.

"We owe it to the boys, even if not to each other," Ron said.

"Let me think about it," I said.

I went back inside and found the boys huddled together on the sofa. They looked unbearably worried, still locked in on the movie. "Scary," said Jesse, pointing to the TV. By now Jiminy Cricket was singing and Pinocchio was a real boy, the frightening parts over. Scary, he insisted. It was as if they had picked up the first tremors of the earthquake that would destroy their world, like frightened animals sensing the ground move under their feet. I flicked the TV off, gathered them in a big hug, and then led them upstairs. It took a while to get them into bed.

Finally I called "Annie [Anne, my sister]." "I did it, but I didn't get anywhere," I said. "Now Ron wants to do counseling," I said.

"That's good," Anne said. "Isn't it?" I was crying again.

"I don't know," I gulped. "I feel like I failed. I don't think counseling will really help. Does this mean I can't ever get divorced?"

"No," she said. "You can still get divorced if you need to. But this won't hurt, even if you do end up having to leave. This is good, this is forward motion. It's okay."

Ron moved into the attic that night, in deference to the seriousness of my feelings. I got into our big bed, which felt wider and private now that it was mine alone, and tried to calm my shaking body. I couldn't imagine how I was going to do it.

Just Too Different

Anne was right, counseling did help, although it didn't bring us to the place we expected. We found a stern, no-nonsense psychiatrist with a wealth of experience counseling troubled couples, and he quickly forced us to own up to our problems and disappointments. Each Wednesday Ron and I would drive together to his office, hardly knowing what to say to each other, then sit in the deep sofas and be surprised by what the other would reveal. The process was like peeling off skin without benefit of anesthesia, but gradually our problems began to surface. Some of it, many of the big things, seemed intractable. We were just too different, our needs and expectations too divergent. We had worn each other out. In the spirit of improvement, however, he encouraged us to do more things together, just the two of us.

By now we were barely comfortable just sitting in the car together, but one evening in April, when the cherry blossoms were at their peak, I talked Ron into a twilight walk around the tidal basin after our counseling session. The cherry blossoms, so beautiful yet so fragile and brief, held a special place in my heart. Every year we were in Washington, my family would make a pilgrimage to see the trees, walking clear around the tidal basin and often sharing a picnic under the flowers. As an adult I had continued the tradition, but usually with friends or by myself. Ron and I had never walked among them together. Now, I needed to see if we could do this small thing. Ron protested at first, saying we should get back to the baby-sitter and the boys, but he finally agreed. It was a lovely night but the traffic was fierce, the wait for a parking space long. When we got out, Ron walked sullenly a few steps ahead of me, always just out of reach, bothered by something in the counseling session and frustrated that I had insisted on this rite. I was hurt that he couldn't enjoy the walk, but I looked at the trees and the happy crowd and told myself that the first try would be the hardest. Finally, we got in the car and went home.

The Beginning of the End

But there another disaster awaited us: The sitter had locked herself out of the house with the boys and had called a locksmith to get in when we didn't show up right after our session. The locksmith was expensive, and the door had been damaged. Ron was furious with the sitter, but he soon turned his frustration on me. It was all my fault—the door, the counseling, the walk around the damn cherry trees. I listened to him rage at me and felt myself move away, off to a distant spot. I didn't need to be here anymore. I didn't have to hear this. I could choose whether I stayed. It was several hours before things settled down enough to go to bed, but before I did, I took off my wedding ring and put it in the bottom of my jewelry box. I couldn't do it anymore. My mother had been right—the forgiveness had run out. Everything had run out—my patience, my love, my hope. I cried myself to sleep, but somehow I felt better. I knew that the end could start now.

I woke up the next morning and got out the list of things I would need to do to get divorced, the one I had written so early in my marriage: talk to a lawyer, divide up the books, pack my things, tell my parents. Rip up my life—nothing to it.

Telling the Family

I was so frightened of going public with my divorce that it took me months to build up the courage to tell my parents. I couldn't say why—I knew they would be understanding and supportive—but whenever I imagined it, a feeling of shame rose in the back of my throat.

Now, though, I needed them. I didn't dare tell Ron it was really over unless I had them there as a backup, in case I needed to move in with them for a few days or take the kids to them in an emergency. What kind of emergency it might be I didn't have any idea, I just felt I needed them on alert. At home, life continued on its jerky course: Ron and I attending the counseling sessions but sharing less and less, the children nervous with the obvious tension between us. Anne was planning a visit east, and my mother and my younger sister and I were to meet her for a weekend in the resort town of Cape May, New Jersey. We had never been away together, just the four of us Swallow girls, and were excited at the prospect. We imagined the weekend spent walking the beach, climbing the lighthouse, sharing tea in quaint little shops, but now I had other plans. I called Annie one evening a few weeks before the trip and told her I had decided to go ahead with the divorce and that I planned to tell Mom the weekend we would be in Cape May. "I need you there," I told her. "I can't tell her by myself."

I could hear Anne sigh all the way from California, but all she said was, "Okay, sweetie. Just warn me a few minutes before you do. At least give me a moment to brace myself."

So a few weeks later, as we sat sharing a bottle of wine in our room at the inn in Cape May, I gave Anne a small signal, took a deep breath, and blurted it out. "Mom, Pen, I have something really important to tell you." They looked up, surprised, unexpecting. I felt as if I was lighting a fuse, starting something that would someday explode. I knew I was changing everything, but I pushed ahead. "I need to divorce Ron," I said simply. "It's over. I can't do it anymore." The I looked at Annie and burst into tears. She wrapped her arms around me and held me until I could speak again. I could barely look at my mother, I felt so overwhelmed by guilt. I had failed at the most important job of my life, the job she had schooled me for, the sacred task of wife and mother. I was supposed to be the support, the keeper of the hearth. Now I was taking a jackhammer to it, cracking it open so I could escape. I hadn't been able to hold it together through thick and thin, through sickness and health. I was giving up.

My mother sat quietly for a moment, then said the one thing I needed to hear. "I understand," she said, leaning forward to squeeze my hand. "I understand why you married Ron and I understand why you need to leave him."

Later that evening, after the tears and questions and talk, we sat around a table in a restaurant and my mother said: "I can't believe how strong you girls are. I don't know where you get it." Indeed. We just looked at each other and smiled.

Getting a Lawyer

Now that I had told my family, the process had to move forward. It wasn't fair for everyone to know more than Ron. When I got back to Washington, I screwed up my courage and called the lawyer. I had gotten his name from an old friend of my parents, who assured me he was competent and understanding, but it hardly helped. Spending money for legal advice meant this was really happening; it was like pushing the start button on some big, unwieldy machine, a machine that could easily lurch out of control. The man seemed harmless on the phone, however, so a few days later I went in for an interview, shaky and girlish in my uneasiness. He was older, mild-mannered, and slightly bumbling, and—as it turned out—more intent on reassuring me than dispensing the best legal advice. I explained the situation, then said I planned on being the custodial parent and staying in the house, but that I would happily give Ron generous visitation rights. He just nodded, as if that was how all divorces happened. He didn't point out that, as I later learned, custody or visitation wasn't mine to "give" to the boys' father, that Ron had the same rights to custody that I had. Instead he told me what I could expect in terms of child support as the custodial parent, went over some basic finances, and then said I didn't need to worry, the boys and I were going to be just fine. "Children are happy if their mommy is happy," he said, patting my hand. "Do you have a boyfriend?"

"No," I said, flushing with the implications of the question.

"Well, go out and find yourself a date. An attractive young woman like you could do with some fun."

I left in a daze. Dates? Fun? That was the farthest thing from my mind. And I didn't feel young and attractive, I felt fat and middle-aged, though I was only thirty-seven. His urging left an unpleasant taste on my tongue, but the rest of the conversation had been reassuring. It didn't seem as if there would be problems with the custody issue, and the child support numbers were better than I had expected. Maybe I could actually do this without going into the poorhouse.

The Final Decision

There was only one thing left to do: tell Ron and the kids. The years of fantasizing, of reading about divorce and weighing the costs, the years of looking at my children and worrying about their future, those countless hours had all led, somehow, to this place, this perch at the edge of the cliff. It was now.

I decided to tell Ron at our next marital counseling session. I was afraid to be alone with him when I did it.

I went home and packed up my most precious possesions, the silver and the ceramic teapot my grandmother had given me and several other breakables, then took them over to my best friend's place. I didn't want them in the house if Ron got angry and suddenly started throwing things. Sandy had listened for years as I had spun my daily troubles into stories, and she understood instinctively why I needed to leave the box in her care, but she seemed worried about me.

"You seem a bit agitated," Sandy said, eyeing me closely as we stashed the box in her basement. "Are you sure you're okay?"

"Well, I'm just nervous. I don't know what Ron will do," I said, pacing around. I could barely stand still.

"Look," she said softly. "I think this will be hard and I think it will be upsetting, but I don't think anything bad is going to happen."

I went home and looked around, trying to talk my panic down to a low hum. Was there anything else I really needed to protect? I packed a small bag, like the one I had taken to the hospital when I gave birth to my children, and stuffed it in the front-hall closet, in case I needed to get out in the middle of the night. I looked around the house, suddenly worried about weapons. No guns, thank God, but there were some nice kitchen knives. I took them downstairs and hid them behind a stack of paint cans in Ron's shop. There were some lethal-looking tools around, but my reason got the better of me. I probably didn't need to hide those. All was ready. I went back upstairs and made dinner for the boys, my hands shaking.

"I Can't Do It Anymore"

We drove down to our counseling session together that evening just as usual, but we both knew the process was unraveling. The last several sessions had been rocky, angry, accusatory. We sat down and within a few minutes I said I had reached a decision. I looked at Ron. "I can't do it anymore. I've talked to a lawyer. We have to get divorced."

Ron sat in the corner of his sofa and said nothing.

The counselor looked at me, unfazed. He asked us both to talk a bit about how that made us feel, but we could barely sit in the room together. Ron seemed beyond words. We finished early, and I don't even remember if we drove home together. I don't see how we could have.

When I got home I busied myself putting the children to bed, then went downstairs to talk with Ron, braced for the anger and the shouting, the next round in the battle. But he wasn't there. He had gone next door to talk with some trusted neighbors. I sat in the living room looking out the window at the familiar street and our yard, thinking about this home and the painful years we had lived here together. It was over, finally over. After a while the husband of the couple Ron was visiting called me. "We can't believe this, Wendy," he said. "Please think about what you are doing." I knew this man and I liked him, but his words made my hackles rise. As if I could do this without having thought it through, without years of agonized indecision, without trying to parse every outcome, every eventuality. Think about it, he suggested. "No," I remember saying. "I've thought about it plenty." I must have sounded like a coldhearted bitch, but I was offended by his request, by the implication that this was some sort of impulsive act. "It's over," was all I had left to say.

That night I slept on the floor in the kids' bedroom. It was the only part of the house that still felt like home.

Husband's Affair Is First Step on Road to Divorce

Mary Stuart

At the age of thirty-eight, Mary Stuart had already been married and divorced once and believed that she was ready for a lasting relationship. She met and married the man she expected to stay with for the rest of her life.

At one point, she began to notice changes in her husband's behavior and in the way he dressed. Then he sent her on a vacation without him, and he took a trip without her. She suspected he was involved with someone else and began to investigate, eventually discovering love letters mixed in with papers in his office. She did not confront her husband, but rather kept that information to herself, attempting to patch the marriage back together. Couples counseling turned into an "exit interview," where they began to disengage from one another in a civilized manner. Even after these discussions, it was still a long time before she was finally ready to pick up and leave the marriage. In this essay, she outlines her second marriage from beginning to end, describing the slow process of coming to the realization that the relationship was over.

I'd successfully navigated through a first marriage, a divorce, and into subsequent relationships which I thought were, once again, going to be my one, my all, my everything. When I married the second time, at the age of thirty-eight, I was convinced it was going to be the last—and lasting—relationship.

Mary Stuart, *Cut Loose: (Mostly) Older Women Talk About the End of (Mostly) Long-Term Relationships*. Piscataway, NJ: Rutgers University Press, 2006.

He was the salt of the earth, stable as they come. He was learning the details of running his family business (and later became the business owner). He adored me. He had never been married, a fact at the time I thought was positive, but which I later realized was a problem for us because I rode the adjustment period with much less concern than he did. He had principles. I know he had principles because he told me all about them. I was in awe. He had more ethics and values than I did. He thought so, too, because he told me quite clearly the third week after our wedding that if I ever cheated on him I could expect to be put out onto the front lawn with nothing but my toothbrush. Maybe not even the toothbrush. He was quite firm about this point because he felt I might cheat on him. We'd had a couple of rough spots during our dating years and once, when we broke up, I had dated others. There was some overlap when we started to see each other again, which he had considered cheating. Back then, I fancied myself a fairly intelligent woman. The thought did cross my mind that I wasn't the one we needed to worry about because his intensity on the subject was so over the top. Of course, I pushed that thought aside and became Mrs. Goody Two-Shoes for the next sixteen years. Like Caesar's wife, I was so above reproach I bored even me. Along the way I failed to notice the adoration's slow disappearance. My husband told me often that I didn't know what I was talking about, that I was opinionated, that other people didn't like my opinions, and he gave me the impression I should just shut up. So I did. With his constant reminders of all my faults on a regular basis over the years, I managed to lose my voice and sink into despair. I gave up all my opinions. I deferred and demurred and otherwise backed off. Later he complained that I never had an opinion about anything and that I left all decisions up to him, which he felt was burdensome.

Can we talk? How crazy making is that?

Sinking Into Depression

Let me back up a bit. First of all, my ex-husband is not a bad man. He and I simply became embroiled in a horrible möbius loop of a marriage that twisted and snaked around on itself in such intricacy that neither one of us could figure out how to exit the morass we'd created. Lack of effective communication leads to such messes. And how could a "fairly intelligent" woman who had a career (as a therapist, for God's sake), and a life, sink into such a pit of despair, and how could she abdicate all her power?

Good question. I've given that a lot of thought since the breakup some ten years ago. I've come to the conclusion that it was very like Chinese water torture—drip drip drip—and day after day, week after week, year after year, I gave up chunks of myself. I hardly noticed the pieces falling off until one morning, about nine or ten years into the marriage, I didn't want to get out of bed because I couldn't find myself; I rolled over and didn't feel my body on the sheets. I thought for one wild moment that I had disappeared and become a disembodied mind lost somewhere in the ether, but no, I was only having a massive anxiety attack. So I did what any red-blooded American, depressed and anxious woman would do. I turned over, pulled the sheet over my head, and went back to sleep. I had great hopes that when I woke up I would somehow reincarnate into my late and sorely missed self.

That craziness went on for some time. I didn't tell my then-husband what was happening to me because I was afraid of his withering contempt, or at least what I perceived as such. I figured if I told him I was depressed and anxious he would think I was crazy, and he did not like "crazy" people, so I had to avoid that label at all costs. In fact, I wasn't crazy, but I *was* crazed, like a clay pot with cracks deep in its infrastructure. Crazed. Cracked. Commensurate behavior was about to ensue.

Noticing Her Husband Has Changed

I felt that his attentions had been directed away from our marriage for some time, but whenever I asked about his new behavior he asked, "What new behavior?" I hunkered down and thought about his new clothes (he hated to shop) and the fact that he left the house every morning with a quart of aftershave splashed into every available pore. Then there was the way his face lit up whenever he was around a certain woman in his office, and how warm his voice became on the phone whenever they spoke. I calculated she was only about five years younger than I, and lulled myself into thinking she couldn't possibly be the typical younger, other woman. There were also the clichéd evening absences due to "work" and other oddities, but I remembered that conversation about infidelity three weeks into our marriage and thought there was no way he would be unfaithful. He might want to leave, he might not want to go to marriage counseling (he didn't believe in psychology), but he wouldn't cheat. He had values. How was I to know he'd forgotten the very conversation he initiated? And I mean *completely* forgotten, as if it had been erased from his memory. It seemed he had his own black hole to deal with.

Ignoring "The Pebbles"

By now you must be asking yourself what the hell was wrong with me. Was I too stupid to live? In a word, yes. I chose to ignore what Oprah calls "the pebbles" that fall on you long before the rocks and the big boulder squash you flat.

But wait! There was more stupidity! He sent me off on a trip (by myself) that I had wanted to take (with him) for a long time. He convinced me that I would enjoy this trip by myself because he wasn't interested in my destination, and when I came back he would take his own vacation to a place I wasn't interested in. I knew by then that something was up and I was frantic to reconnect, but I was floating down that famous river in Egypt, De Nial, and I shut off any notion that he might be unfaithful. I hoped the time apart would help us (that was the stupid part). When we both returned from our trips, the distance between us had grown colder and larger. I couldn't stand it anymore, so I asked for an explanation. We made a date to talk. He took me to a restaurant and commenced the Big Dump. In public, I suppose that was so I wouldn't create a scene. He needn't have worried. In the dutiful habit of being Mrs. Goody Two-Shoes, I bit my lip, fought back tears, and listened as he explained he "needed some space" (I swear, that's what he said). He told me he was thinking about leaving, which I interpreted to mean that he hadn't yet decided, so while I took an out-of-body trip somewhere way past Jupiter, Mrs. Goody Two-Shoes took over and told him that I respected his need for "space." It was an oh-so-civilized meeting, and he sighed in relief and moved out to our summer cabin the next day.

However, a niggling little voice in the back of my head was scratching on the walls of its jail where I'd consigned it years ago in the hope it would go away. I felt the scratch, ignored it. Then I heard faint sounds. I tried to ignore the whole sorry mess I called my mind, but soon I had a full-blown harpy in my head screaming at me that I was about to be done in and I'd better by God get out of my pit of despair, back away from the event horizon of that yawning black hole, and get my butt in gear so as to save said butt from ruin.

So what about that cracked behavior? For a long time I couldn't tell anyone except my closest friends just how crazy I was about to become, but from the distance of some years I look back and have to laugh. However serious I thought it was at that time, I see now how utterly comical it really was. Not to mention banal.

Finding Proof of His Other Relationship

Danger causes the brain to flood itself and the body with feel-good natural drugs, and they produce a high second to none.

They also produce feelings of empowerment and strength. For the next four months, before I moved out of our house, I felt like Wonder Woman. My behavior was still cracked, as I will relate below, but I felt great. I had The Power, baby, because by then I'd found proof of his other relationship, a discovery I kept to myself. My rationale for that was twofold: one, I hoped the whole mess would blow over, no harm, no foul; and two, if I kept my own counsel he would not have to face the fact every time he looked at me that I knew what he'd done. From my experience counseling others I had observed that some couples survived the initial infidelity but that the offending party, statistically equal between men and women, often couldn't get past his/her guilt and the relationship broke up anyway. I wanted to avoid that particular pitfall. In counseling couples, I knew each case was unique, but the one outstanding piece of behavior that seemed to appear in all of them was that for a couple to successfully get past infidelity both of them had to rise above their own flaws. In the case of the offender, getting over guilt was the hardest. With the offendee, anger and resentment were the barriers to successful reengagement.

In the sixteen years we were married I had done the unthinkable, the one thing I always advised women in my counseling practice never to do, and I do mean never. I gave up control of our finances and had no idea what our financial status was apart from our everyday lifestyle. I had done this for several reasons. One, I didn't want to make waves. Two, I hoped he had more knowledge than I did in terms of investments. It never occurred to me that I should worry about it. After all, we were in the same boat, weren't we?

The harpy kicked in again, this time bellowing that I'd better check it out. There is nothing like a good survival scare to get a body, however depressed, into motion. The only problem was that all our financial records were kept at his business office. I couldn't let him know how suspicious I was, thanks to the attorney, newly and secretly hired, who exhorted me to keep quiet until I got my hands on the financial records. The harpy cackled her agreement. The bitch was back. I had been one of those wives who held titular corporate offices in the family business. The office building was fitted with an alarm system that consistently went off for no discernible reason and annoyed the neighbors and I had a key so I could take care of that problem in my husband's absence. I had returned his key to him when we finished our solitary and separate trips, but I had had a spare made for future absences. I looked at the key daily and thought about it for a while.

Becoming a Cat Burglar at His Office

Finally, I decided that on nights when I was certain he was at the summer cabin, I would take up a new career. I became a cat burglar. Of course, I had legal access to the office and our financial records, so I wasn't really a burglar, but the drama of it all kicked in and I went for it. Please remember cracked and crazed.

I decided the best time to cat burgle was around one or two o'clock in the morning. I parked the car in a dark spot at the back of the building, and dressed all in black (yes, really), I let myself in to the office and proceeded with a routine I developed over several visits. Blinds down and closed. Only rear office lights on. A quick rustle through the file cabinet that held all our financial records. And then the tedious chore of copying documents on paper I brought along so the office supply would not be noticeably smaller. An hour or so, no longer, then lights out. Blinds back up. And I was gone, like the spies say, in the wind.

It was during one of those forays that I stumbled over the proof—love letters, tucked in with the financial records. That was the night that I fell way past the event horizon and into the black hole. It's one thing to have suspicions, to be uneasy and uncertain, to question, even to go looking. It's entirely another to fall into the pudding of the proof, a slimy, sloppy, gooey place where drowning occurs. And so I did, for one night. Drown. The night I stayed up and read every single letter. The night I read they had discussed leaving their respective spouses for each other. The night I read how lucky they felt for having this rare and unusual love, this great passion. The night I read about their activities and realized many of my memories had to be realigned to fit the facts, not his lies. I felt like puking, but I didn't. Instead, I grieved the loss of my marriage, and I grieved for my then-husband because I knew that the light of romantic love had blinded him to any reality. Romantic love feels great. I can recommend the experience. But as a friend of mine once observed, it lasts approximately ninety days; on the ninety-first day the first load of reality arrives like an unwelcome relative. For people who are unfaithful, that drug-induced high with their new partners can last until their current marriage breaks up. I'm no expert (who is?), but I believe that long-term marriages contain a combination of intermittent romantic love (no one can sustain that initial level over many years), friendship, spirituality, and what I call a commitment to the commitment. When it gets rough (and it always does), there has to be a mutual agreement to hang in there at least long enough to work through it—one way or another—*before* moving on to someone else.

Attempting to Follow Him

The craziness didn't stop. Soon after my discovery of the infidelity, my car was in the shop for repairs and I acquired a loaner car. Driving home I realized no one would recognize the car, "no one" being my then-husband and his new honey. An irresistible urge to find them together overwhelmed me. I had copies of their letters so I didn't need further proof, but I had a driving, almost physical need to see them in each other's company with my own eyes. It was fall, it was cold, and it was raining. I created a different physical profile for myself by stuffing my hair under a stocking cap and wearing nondescript clothes. I headed out to find them that evening. My ex had been spending a lot of time at our summer cabin trying to find himself and his space, so I figured they would probably go there for privacy. I went to his office building and skulked around outside trying to determine if he'd left. I had the half-baked notion of following him. Skulking around his office wasn't easy because the building was isolated and located in a large open space and there was no place to park unnoticed. After making endless loops driving around, I realized I had missed him. I headed out for the summer cabin, which was located, with a few other cabins, down a dead-end gravel road. Occupants of the cabins could hear cars coming half a mile away, so just to be on the safe side I parked a mile away and slogged through the rain and mud and, did I mention, the dark of night, like a postal carrier determined to let nothing stay her course. Of course no one was there. When you're crazed, no one is ever where they're supposed to be.

Demoralized, I headed for home and . . . there he was. He'd decided to spend that night at our house. As I dragged my sorry butt in out of the weather, dripping wet, he just stared at me. And at the "new car" sitting in the carport. I explained about the car being serviced and mumbled something about my disheveled self. I needn't have worried. He was so uninterested in me I could have said I just returned from a rough flight to the moon in the shuttle and he would have nodded, uh-huhed and disappeared somewhere in the house still, no doubt, trying to find his space.

After that dark and stormy night (I felt like Snoopy on top of his doghouse, writing the quintessential novel), I told my husband it would only be courteous to let me know when he planned on spending the night or nights at the house. After all, I couldn't barge in on him at the cabin, could I? (When had I become so good at walking the balance beam of the slippery moral line?) He agreed, and I swallowed my hypocrisy whole.

Trying to Patch Marriage Back Together

After that episode, somehow I returned to semi-sanity, bucked up, and resolved to patch our marriage back together. Why throw away sixteen years of marriage? Wasn't that worth saving? I shoved the ever-present and vocally abusive harpy back in her cell and told her to shut up. I found a marriage counselor and made an appointment.

The counseling turned out to be exit counseling, or what is termed "counseling for closure," because after two sessions I realized he wasn't thinking about leaving, he'd already left the building. Exit counseling exists for the sole purpose of letting the couple disengage in a civilized fashion, that is, encouraging them to do an autopsy on their relationship and to make peace with the fact that it is over. At its best, it helps prevent acrimonious divorces and custody battles. I didn't want to flog a deceased relationship into tatters. However, I had a few things to say, so I requested he stay for two more sessions so I could unload everything I had on my chest, which was considerable. That's when I discovered he'd forgotten all about his threatening conversation in the early weeks of our marriage. I was dumbfounded. And angry, mostly with myself because I also remembered I'd said at that time he might be the one we should worry about. One day I may learn to listen to that small voice and thereby avert disaster. That was not one of those days. I also requested he stay through the holiday season, a request he readily agreed to. I suspect he was feeling merciful because it was plain that I was unraveling just a tad around the edges. However, I rallied because . . . drum roll . . . I knew something he didn't know. I knew his secret and he didn't know I knew it. This was the four-month period in which I morphed into Wonder Woman. I was strong. I was invincible. Hear me roar. I was still just a bit cracked.

Throwing Herself a Goodbye Party

In that state, I decided to throw myself a good-bye party because I was determined that sometime after the holidays were over I would move out of our house to a larger city some distance away from our small town. That decision came from not wanting to live alone in an isolated rural setting, which was where our house was located. I thought that I would probably never see our joint married friends again and I wanted a last time together. It was a different kind of farewell party because nobody except me knew it *was* a farewell party. My soon-to-be-ex and I smiled, served, circulated, hosted, poured drinks, refreshed drinks, made small and big talk and otherwise looked like the glowing golden couple all our friends perceived us to be. I had a really good time. I said good-bye in my head, noticed all the small things, and was, as the Zen folks say, fully in the moment. It's hard to describe the powerful feelings that ensue when you're the only person in the room who knows what's really happening. When I told some of those people after my husband and I separated what had gone down (I was surprised some of them actually remained my friends), most of them were astonished. Some sensed something was wrong, just not the details. Some thought it was a hoot I threw myself an anonymous farewell party. I had such a good time I decided to do it again, this time at my husband's annual Christmas party in mid-December. I'd lost about thirty pounds during the previous three months (stress, anxiety, and depression are better than amphetamines for weight loss) and, if I do say so myself, I was looking pretty good. I owned, but previously could not get into, a stunning red silk Anne Klein suit, which now fit. I wore a sexy black lace teddy underneath the jacket, slinky stockings, and high-heeled shoes. I looked hot. More to the point, I felt hot. I should mention here that no one dressed up for this annual Christmas party, but I didn't care. I wanted all those people, including the other woman, to remember the boss's soon-to-be-ex-wife the night she looked like a million bucks in that red suit, before she disappeared in a puff of smoke. I don't know that any of them remember me at all, of course, but I know they noticed me that night.

Going Through the Motions for the Holidays

Christmas was pretty dismal because we weren't telling the family anything. Going through the motions was difficult. Fortunately, there were no children to worry about. That left New Year's Eve, which was simply a disaster. It had been my favorite holiday after Christmas because it was one of the few times we dressed up and went dancing. Or at least, we watched other people dance because my one, my all, my everything didn't like to dance and toward the end of our marriage took to a flat refusal when I suggested it. I admit I should have thought ahead to the midnight event, but I didn't. I had not expected a kiss, but I thought a friendly hug would have been civilized considering we were with two other couples. Instead, he abandoned me in the middle of the festivities and took a chair by a column in the ballroom, chin on his chest, deep in thought. I stood like the ninny I was, alone in the middle of the room, flabbergasted. And furious, Don't love me anymore? OK. Want your own space? OK. Humiliate me in public in front of friends? I don't *think* so. Happily, everyone was so caught up in kissing each other no one noticed our complete lack of contact. It was one of those clarifying moments when you know absolutely what comes next and what you have to do. I took control of my future and later that night I told him he'd made it clear to me it was time I moved on. He probably wondered what took me so long. By January 15 I was out and in an interim apartment. I was in that apartment for a year and a half while the divorce ground down to its inevitable end. I stayed with the therapist as I tried to get over beating myself up for being a failure and to come to terms with what my part was in the demise of the marriage. In addition, I read like a mad woman everything I could get my hands on that dealt with my current predicament. I found a great deal of reading material, but there were only a few things that resonated with me. . . .

Moving On

My life has moved on, as lives always do. Being single and older ain't for sissies. Dating? Help me. The entire singles' scene seems to be geared toward the younger set. Being dumped at sixteen is different from being dumped at fifty-two. When you're young the possibilities for recovery are endless, and the next romance is usually just around the corner. The percentages for finding a significant other begin to shrink exponentially as we age, or at least they have for me. Maybe I'm pickier than I was at sixteen, maybe I'm more jaded, or maybe I'm not as desirable to the opposite sex as I once was. The thought of living in my future alone isn't always happy, but I have friends, a couple of careers, and a life. I gave up daydreaming that my ex-husband had been drugged and was struggling to free himself from his new relationship. I tried very hard to fight the notion that I'm terminally special and therefore impossible to give up, which alternated with feelings of ineptitude and worthlessness. Finding the balance has been my goal.

The final act to my relationship came about eight years after the official fizzle when my ex-husband asked me to help him obtain an annulment through the Catholic Church. Since neither one of us was Catholic, but his new significant other was, I figured a marriage was in the near future. It was the last straw. Although by that time I had moved away geographically, I realized that our every communication raised the specter of the marriage, a ghost that clung to me like the clutching vegetation of a swamp-thing. I didn't want to help him at all, and according to the Catholic Church precepts, I discovered he could obtain the annulment without any assistance from me. However, what he wanted was to do it the easy way (which meant he needed my help). While fuming to a friend one day she asked me if I wanted him to go away. I said, emphatically, yes. Then, she said, why don't you just give him what he wants? She had a point. But I had one, too, and that was that my voice was going to be heard in the process, the voice I'd lost in order to keep the peace. I told him what I remembered about my first divorce, and then told him I was severing all communication with him. We had no children to co-parent, there were no ties between us, either financial or emotional, and I did not want to talk to him, see him, e-mail him, or communicate with him in any way one more minute of my life. I cut him loose and requested, politely, that he return the favor. He tried to re-engage me several times, and then finally stopped. I haven't heard from him in almost three years, and do not know the aftermath of the annulment (which was granted). He could be married. He could be dead. What I felt then, and feel now, is a "click" of disengagement and a corresponding feeling of freedom which I can only illustrate with the feeling you get when you take a deep gulp of air after surfacing from beneath a deep body of water.

Pornography and Other Women Entice Husband Away from Marriage

Noelle Quinn

Noelle Quinn's husband was busy and away from home a lot, using "work-related engagements" and other excuses to explain his absences. He accompanied her on what was supposed to be a romantic trip together, but he wasn't really present. Eventually, Quinn realized he was into pornography. When confronted, he admitted it. Over time, she also discovered that he was having affairs with a number of other women. In this series of vignettes, Quinn describes some of the occasions of her husband's infidelity that led up to their divorce.

I tuck our three-year-old into bed and sit down to nurse our newborn. [My husband] Dan is washing the dishes. Then he sits down with me. I look forward to the evenings together. He says he has to go back to the office. His job seems time-consuming and demanding, but when a pastor calls asking him to speak on relationships at a weekend retreat, he takes that on too. I question him, expressing frustration, but he brushes it off abruptly. He says I'm not letting him be a man. His comebacks are like a slap in the face, but I can't define the feeling. He showers, then gets in the car and drives away. . . .

Desperate for His Affection

"I need you to plan a special occasion for our big anniversary," I say after the birth of our third child. "Somewhere nice." It sounds like a demand, but it's my way of saying, *I'm desperate for your affection.*

Noelle Quinn, *When He Leaves*. Eugene, OR: Harvest House Publishers, 1998.

I juggle small children and a part-time job, and I need to know: Either he cares for me or he doesn't.

Dan plans a weekend anniversary trip—in connection with his business. He books a cheap flight and a cheaper hotel room. He isn't present emotionally. We spend the first night arguing. *Why is our marriage so difficult?* I keep asking myself. . . .

He Makes Excuses to Be Out of the House

During the day, Dan works from our home. Evenings, he finds a justification to see the "soccer match" at a pub downtown, meet "friends," or take a "photography safari." I wait up for him night after night, always crawling into our empty bed with an eerie ache.

"Give me space," he says when I ask why he avoids me. I blame it on his midlife crisis, his waning business, and my success.

"I'll be in the city all weekend working on a project," Dan informs me.

"Again? Why?" I counter. His two-day trips to a metropolitan area are increasing. "Can't you just do the research here?"

I feel uneasy about the reasons he gives me. . . .

Out-of-Town Trips

"Don't worry about the kids. Have fun," Dan says. He seems delighted each time I leave on a business trip. I'm proud of the way he jumps in and takes care of the house and girls. He seems proud of me and my job. I never worry about things when I go away.

But this time, I wake up in my hotel room the first night and feel a strong presence in the room. I don't often get on my knees, but this time I do. For several hours, I pour out my heart, compelled to pray for our marriage. I feel God is doing something good at last.

Home again after an exciting ten-day trip, I can't wait to see my family and tell them about it. I believe things will be different with Dan and me. But he isn't at the airport to meet me. Half an hour later, he arrives, acting as if nothing is wrong. I'm in tears. He belittles me in front of our girls, blaming me for upsetting them.

Two days later, when we host a dinner party with friends to show pictures of my trip, his attention centers on a certain woman, a neighbor. He keeps pouring drinks for her and leaves "for the office" as soon as she makes her exit. . . .

For our twentieth wedding anniversary we plan a week-long trip to a romantic destination, though things are difficult between us. One week before we are to leave, Dan tells me we can't afford to go. I'm furious, but I bridle my emotions. I know I'll ruin what little relationship we have if I blow up.

We spend a weekend at a hotel close to home. Dan doesn't touch me or talk to me on the trip. I confront him with his lack of presence. He says, "I'm fine. I'm here. I'm enjoying myself. Why can't you let me be?"

I feel invisible in black lace.

Realizing Her Husband Is Into Pornography

Working in the quiet of my home office, I sense a heavy blanket fall over me. *I know*. I know Dan is into pornography on trips to the city and in our home when I'm away.

"Isn't that true?" I ask when I call him at the office.

He sighs. "Yes," he says.

"You need to get counseling," I plead. "Deal with this. Pour out your gut to somebody. Get help."

He agrees.

Other Women

Several days later, I find by the bathroom sink a love letter posted from out of town. It's addressed to Dan, alluding to time in bed. When I ask him to explain, he looks both defiant and exposed.

"She didn't really mean this," he says. "You're taking it out of context."

For the first time, I know without a doubt he is lying. This is not an overactive imagination. Truth is there in black-and-white. He grabs the letter from my hand and leaves.

After a flurry of phone calls that Dan always answers, he says finally. "There's something I have to tell you."

I brace myself.

He spills out details of an affair with another man's wife—not the person who had written the love letter.

"It didn't mean anything," he says. "She's in love with me now, but I don't love her. I'm cutting the whole thing off."

What is going on? How many are there? I wonder, unable to articulate my despair and his denial. My heart feels like a knife has been plunged into it. *I can't believe this is happening.*

"I'm not going to be depressed anymore," Dan tells me. "I'm leaving."

"Why?" I plead. "We can work this out. I love you. I want to stay married. For us. For the children. I can forgive you. I can change if you want me to. I can meet your needs if I just know what they are: kinky sex, anything."

"No. I've always needed something you're not."

"There's *another* woman?"

"No," he says.

"A man?" I manage a laugh.

"I just have to leave."

I beg him to stay just one more week—until our daughter's holiday performance. He agrees. . . .

He Admits To Frequent Infidelity

Weeks later, Dan and I talk about how to tell our oldest child about our breakup. She is spending a semester abroad. I look straight into his eyes and blurt out words that erupt from my lips. "And I know about all your prostitutes and old girlfriends." *I can't believe I said that. I did not know any such thing; where did that come from?*

Dan glares at me. "Have you been talking to my counselor?"

"No." I say, still shocked by what I had said.

Numbness envelops me as Dan admits infidelity starting with our first year of marriage. "I had to do it," he says, adding. "I'm still a Christian." He leaves. I stay at my bedside for hours, stunned, immoble.

Doing Better

A year before Dan left, I had christened the new year "A Year of Light." I wrote my prayer requests, including skylights for our home, in my journal. Little did I realize then how my prayer for light would be answered. Not in the way I expected! Exposure brought nauseating waves of pain and rage. My childhood dream to dance stories on a beautiful stage burst like a bubble. And that dollhouse? Someone else did come and move things around despite the fact that I was there first.

I crawled, trudged, and climbed through that year. I determined to feel the deep rage deeply, then leave it behind. Out of sheer will to survive, I forgave—in increments. I learned to look deeper and harder and to own the truth, no matter how painful. Today I know truth is worth clinging to, because it set me free.

One morning an acquaintance told me she was moving across the street from me. I'd seen her eyes swollen recently, the way mine looked last year. I said, "Look, if you're going through what I've just been through. I'm so sorry."

She said, "Well, how are you doing?"

"Oh, so much better," I told her.

She sighed with relief and said. "That's what I need to hear."

Steps to a Peaceful Ending

David J.

David J. recalls the day when his wife sat him down during a walk in the woods and told him their marriage was about to end. He outlines five steps that helped him towards the peaceful ending of their marriage. The steps are:

1. Couple's counseling that taught them how to communicate
2. Having a breakthrough "moment" when he realized that he was a worthwhile person even without his spouse
3. Attending men's groups for support
4. Agreeing that their daughter's well-being was most important
5. Deciding that he would not use money to express his anger

Some memories don't fade, even when we want them to. It was the Sunday after Thanksgiving, 1990, when my wife asked me to take a walk with her. A few minutes into the woods, she stopped and sat by a favorite boulder and told me in so many words that our marriage was about to end. Two years later, to the day, we received our final divorce decree.

The journey that began with that walk in the woods is one I continue today. That first year was easily the worst of my life—full of grief, anger, despair, and confusion. Certainly the acute pain of those early years is gone, but it's not hard to locate the scar, that place where, like an old injury in damp weather, I can still feel the dull ache of loss.

But my divorce was also a time of genuine awakening, of finding my own identity as if for the first time, and of work-

David J., "One Man's Divorce Journey; A Walk in the Woods," *Voice Male*, winter 2005, p. 10.

ing through the divorce process itself with intention and integrity for both of us. I'd have given anything to have done my self-discovery some other way, but I can honestly say I'm a better man for the experience.

I can point to several steps that led to the peaceful ending of our marriage and the effective beginning of the rest of my life. First, my wife agreed to my request that we try couples' counseling. Second, I had what can only be described as a moment of emotional breakthrough. Third, I began to attend men's groups. Fourth, we were agreed from the start that our daughter, who was 15 at the time, would not be an issue between us. Fifth, I decided at the outset that, however angry I might be at any point, I would not use money as a means to express my anger. And finally, we agreed to use mediation rather than litigation to settle the terms of the divorce.

Couples' Counseling

Though reluctant and skeptical at first, my wife (I'll call her Betsy) agreed to try couples' counseling before deciding whether she could stay in the marriage. In our walk she'd been clear that she wasn't ready to give up on our relationship yet, even though she was just as clearly pulling away. We entered counseling with the full understanding that it might lead us to a decision to end the marriage—though I was equally clear that I was hoping to "save" it. Over the next six or seven months we began to communicate for the first time about the broken places in our marriage. I began to learn the difficult task of uncovering my feelings, feeling those feelings, and talking about them. Eventually we both came to recognize that we had in fact grown so far apart that we couldn't put our marriage back together. After one last attempt via a weekend couples' workshop, we knew it was over. But now it was we who knew, not just one of us. I was not happy with that realization, but I accepted its reality.

The Breakthrough "Moment"

Shortly after the fateful walk, I left on a previously scheduled trip to Florida to pick up a car from my father and drive it home to New Hampshire. As I sat on the plane, half unconscious from lack of sleep, I heard a voice inside me saying, You are a good and a worthwhile person, over and over. And I felt myself believing that, seemingly for the first time in my life. I began to cry, and couldn't stop. Here I was, trapped in an airplane seat, sobbing as quietly as my minimal willpower could manage, and absorbing this simple but life-changing message from . . . where? I didn't know or care where it came from or how it suddenly arose within me; I just knew it was true. In the words of therapist John Wellwood, my heart had broken—open. When, full of hope, I told Betsy about what had happened, she reminded me that I might have changed, but she hadn't. That brought me back to earth in a hurry; there were plenty of tears ahead. But the fact was that I was suddenly, dramatically, in a different place with respect to myself, even if I didn't fully understand it.

Men's Groups

The morning after hearing my marriage might end, I was staring in the mirror and thought, I need to remake myself in my own image. Somehow I understood that I'd been spending my life trying to be what I thought others—especially the women I most cared about—wanted me to be. It may have taken me 47 years, but I was finally figuring out that that wasn't working. And my intuition led me to realize this was about being a man. For as long as I'd given masculinity any thought, from my teens onward, I had rejected the conventional stereotypes of manhood—the implicit violence, the denigration of women, the bravado—but hadn't replaced them with positive images of what it means to be a man. I knew in that moment at the mirror that I needed to connect with other men and explore the question of maleness with them.

By coincidence, an article appeared in a local weekly soon afterward about an organization in Brattleboro [Vermont], called For and About Men, which held monthly forums on men's issues. I contacted one of the organizers, who put me in touch with someone who in turn told me about a group that met in Keene [New Hampshire]. I began attending the group, where I found men I could trust, who would listen as I poured out my heart and my tears, who would hold me in their arms and hearts, and who would affirm my worth and even my courage. Later I formed a group closer to home, with men closer to my own age and life circumstances. I developed real friendships with men—a rarity in my life before then—and learned the meaning of genuine mutual support.

I recognize now what these experiences were doing for me: I was developing my own sense of self that I could present in a relationship, rather than reflect back what I thought someone else wanted from me. That's a continuing journey (with many a step backward as well as forward), but this is where it started. During the separation and divorce, this also meant that I was able to be alone—by myself, with myself—without being lonely. That in turn freed me from the feelings of desperation and dread that had always arisen in me around the possibility of divorce.

Terms of Estrangement

From the beginning, Betsy and I were in complete agreement that our daughter's well-being was of paramount importance. We couldn't avoid the turmoil she would go through over the next couple of years, but we were of one mind that, however we might feel about each other during these struggles, we wouldn't fight about her. Never in the separation and divorce process did either of us criticize the other in conversations with her, nor did we argue about custody or child support. There were many moments when emotions ran high, but our daughter never became a vehicle for expressing them. When

Betsy eventually moved out of our home to her own apartment, she found one about a mile away so our daughter could easily be at either house.

When it became apparent that a formal separation was necessary, I went to an attorney and had a separation agreement drawn up. Money had been an issue in our marriage for some time, spoken and unspoken. Betsy had never taken on a real career, and as a result I was the principal earner for the family. This was not a situation that I'd ever accepted with equanimity, and I had encouraged and even urged Betsy to do more about having a full time job that was both financially and emotionally rewarding. Now we were in a situation where we were setting up separate households, and I was in the unwanted position of having to be the primary supporter of both of them. I wasn't happy about this continuing disparity in our incomes, but I knew I could not and would not use money to punish Betsy or to gain concessions from her in the divorce. It was an easy decision: I knew I couldn't live with myself if I exerted power in this way. In the end, I had to be satisfied with the ethics of my own behavior, and I tried as best I could to act accordingly.

Mediation

When we finally realized the marriage was over, we agreed to try mediation rather than go to our respective lawyers. We weren't fighting each other; at this point sadness rather than anger was the predominant emotion. We each trusted the other to act honestly and considerately, so mediation didn't feel like a risk. Before we started, I asked Betsy to return with me to our couples' therapist for one session, to get our emotional "temperature" and maybe to clear any lingering obstacles to the negotiations we were about to undertake. I don't know if Betsy got anything out of that last session, but I learned something very important: she was scared. She knew very well how limited her earning ability was, and she was genuinely and deeply afraid of ending up in poverty. I came away from that session knowing that I would need to be aware of that fear when money issues came up during mediation.

We contacted the New Hampshire Mediation Center in Concord, who assigned us two volunteer mediators. The Center charged us $60 an hour—far less than even one lawyer, let alone two, would have cost. (Betsy did engage an attorney to advise her during the negotiations, but used her far less than if we'd litigated.) The mediation sessions didn't all go smoothly: my feelings and hers around money issues brought us to some hard spots. It was here that my recognition of her fear eventually helped me move off my position and toward compromise. There were times afterward when I felt I'd conceded too much, where the old resentments about her not having contributed more to our finances during our marriage resurfaced, but during the mediation I was able to see that a few hundred or even a few thousand dollars meant very little in the long run, especially compared to the emotional and financial costs of a contested divorce.

We agreed to an extended period of alimony—four years—but we also agreed that we would have joint legal and physical custody of our daughter, which meant that all my transfer of income to Betsy would be as alimony, not as child support. This was an important distinction, because I was in a higher tax bracket than Betsy, and alimony is deductible from the payer's income and taxable on the payee's income. Child support, on the other hand, is nondeductible, so it would come out after paying my higher tax rate. In our case it meant that more of my income could actually end up in Betsy's hands rather than the government's. We also agreed to a key stipulation: that if either of our financial situations changed significantly, we would renegotiate the terms. The Mediation Center's volunteer lawyers, who reviewed the agreement to identify any areas the court might question, expressed concern about the possible ambiguity of the word "significantly." But we decided we could trust each other well enough to leave it in, and the court accepted it. In fact, we did invoke that clause twice—once when I took a salary cut to change jobs, and again when she became unemployed near the end of the four years.

Avoiding Lawyers

During the mediation, I discovered another invaluable service of the Mediation Center: they sold a booklet that details how to file a divorce pro se—by oneself. Using the mediation agreement as the heart of the documentation—the "stipulations"—I followed their instructions and sample forms to the letter, and a few months later, sans attorney, I stood before a judge and received approval of the agreement.

It's been a dozen years since that piece of paper was signed and sealed. Both of us are settled with other partners. I can't say Betsy and I are friends—we live several hundred miles apart, and our only communications are birthday and holiday cards. And I can't say old resentments have never come up. But I can say my soul not only is intact, but has prospered in these years since that terribly difficult walk in the woods. Finding my heart and voice as a man I can respect has made all the difference.

Chapter 2

The Process of Divorce

Making Custody Decisions

Lorraine Bracco

In this excerpt from actress Lorraine Bracco's book On the Couch, *she discussed the battle with Harvey Keitel over the custody of their daughter, Stella.*

Initially the couple went to a family therapist with the intention of behaving like responsible adults in making custody decisions with Stella's best interests in mind. They reached an agreement where Stella would be living with Bracco, but after a three week visitation with her, Keitel announced that he was keeping Stella and refused to give her back. Bracco had to continually muster legal pressure to enforce the custody plan that had been originally agreed to.

Through lawyers, Harvey [Keitel] and I carved out a legal agreement that I would have custody of [our daughter] Stella, but he would see her frequently, as his schedule permitted. We'd consult each other on every important issue and behave like reasonable, responsible adults. We decided to go together to a highly recommended family therapist, Dr. Harvey Corman, to talk about how we could best assure Stella's wellbeing. Okay so far.

But during our first meeting with Dr. Corman, it seemed that, in Harvey's mind, the only issue was my infidelity and how to break the news of it to Stella. He appeared too angry and hurt to see that our breakup was a long time in the making, and that the best thing we could do for our daughter was to figure out how to move on peacefully.

Dr. Corman discouraged Harvey from talking to Stella about my affair with Eddie [Edward James Olmos], but Harvey kept insisting that the truth was best for everyone. He brushed off my pleas, accusing me of only wanting to protect myself. There was just no reasoning with him. He often said, "You cheated on your daughters and me," as if they were a package that I'd destroyed.

We had wanted Harvey to maintain his relationship with twelve-year-old Margaux [my daughter from a previous marriage] but that didn't work too well, either. She accompanied Stella on a weekend visitation into the city, and returned vowing to never go back—and she never did. She said that Harvey had spent much of the time screaming, and it had been awful. From then on, little Stella would make the trip alone.

"Mommy, why can't Margaux come with me?" Stella whined each time she got ready to go to Harvey's. It was hard enough for a young child to understand why her daddy didn't live with us anymore. It was very hard to explain to her why Margaux wasn't part of the visitation system. We'd always been *one* family, and while Harvey wasn't Margaux's biological father, he'd been the father figure in her life for the last eight years. But now everything had changed.

Disputing the Custody Agreement

In August of 1991 we planned for Stella to spend three weeks with Harvey in L.A. [Los Angeles], where he was filming a movie. I had hoped it would be a good break for her before she started kindergarten in the fall. Margaux was in Paris visiting her father, and I flew out to California with Stella. When we arrived at the house he was renting in Malibu, I immediately saw that this wasn't going to be a cordial exchange. Harvey was happy to see Stella, and gave her a huge hug and kiss, but after she'd run off to her room, he started in on me.

"Harvey, keep it down," I said, worried that his yelling would upset Stella. I knew I had to get out of there before he really erupted. Seeing me just brought out the worst in him.

I found Stella, and kissed her. "You have a good time, honey," I said brightly, faking a smile. She was happy to be in California, and for once she didn't seem to notice the tension.

Harvey followed me out to the car, badgering me all the way. He was full of questions, mostly about Eddie.

"I don't want my daughter around that man," he growled.

"Harvey, Stella has never even met Eddie. Cool it, all right?"

I started to get into the car, but Harvey clamped a hand around my arm and yanked me out. He started shaking me, screaming obscenities. I sensed he was spinning out of control. I was afraid he would hit me. I pulled loose, furious, and got back in the car. He yelled after me, "She's staying with me now. You're not getting her back."

I figured it was just talk, but when the end of August came, Harvey called and announced that he was keeping Stella and registering her in school in the city.

"Harvey, she's already registered in Rockland County. You need to bring her back."

"Make me," he shouted, slamming down the phone.

By this point I had hired Manhattan attorney Jack Zulack to represent me, so I put in a call to him. He talked to Harvey's lawyer and called me back, informing me that Harvey said he wouldn't give Stella back until a court ordered him to.

"That's ridiculous," I said. "We have a legal custody agreement."

Unfortunately, legal agreements are only as good as the willingness of the parties to go along with them. Jack was reluctant to get involved in a lengthy court battle over custody, and so was I. The lawyers were already engaged in a complicated and frustrating effort to reach three separate agreements on custody, child support, and the disposition of our shared property. Harvey seemed determined to make things difficult every step of the way. He finally returned Stella, but only after my lawyer put the pressure on.

Negotiating a Settlement

Liz Perle

Liz Perle's book, Money, a Memoir, *discusses the role of money in all aspects of her life. In this excerpt, she discusses the financial decisions involved in the divorce process. In her case, she decided that it was more important to be happy than to be rich. In order to avoid years of resentful feelings, she had to avoid using money as a weapon and negotiate for the amount she felt that she needed, not for the larger amount that she wished she could have.*

When something is taken away and we feel powerless, we can respond with resignation, acceptance, or stoicism. We can cry, get angry—even vengeful. In my case, every time I wanted to do something or buy something and realized I could no longer afford it, all those emotions washed over me, with a good dash of envy mixed in. As I neared the final negotiations for my divorce, every emotion I ever experienced about money swirled around my meetings with the mediator.

Everyone's divorce is different. But each requires us to put a price on our lives. That means that someone has to assign a value to something that the other spouse has just said they don't want anymore. It's a kind of paradox, one that requires a strong sense of inner worth to lay claim to an outer one.

But I knew one thing for sure: I genuinely wanted to be happy more than I wanted to be rich. I couldn't afford to be envious or spiteful or indirect. To negotiate for my future, I had to relegate all those old money-related behaviors to the sidelines if not permanently exile them. There was something money could buy in my divorce settlement—and that was good feelings. Not his at the expense of mine, or mine at the expense of his. Instead, we were going to have to find a compromise between money as power and money as connection. We were going to have to balance the imperatives of two systems to come up with one workable financial solution.

Being Honest About Her Needs

Above all else, my husband and I had a son in common. I had watched enough people scorch enough earth in divorces to know that all anyone got out of them was ash. Using money as a weapon has long-term repercussions, and neither of us wanted to live with the years of resentment involved. But that meant I was going to have to be completely honest about what I needed—not what I wanted.

Out came the legal pad again. I drew up a detailed budget. I wrote down what I estimated our living expenses would be—average, responsible expenses. I wrote down what I thought I could earn annually. Then, assessing the gap, I asked my husband to contribute toward closing it. Because I had been able to separate out my emotional needs from my financial ones, our negotiations were rational and calm, and we swiftly and very amicably worked out a settlement. I didn't get everything I wanted, and neither did he. But in the end, he felt good, and I felt good. We put a higher value on long-term friendship than we did on short-term economic gain.

Maintaining a Good Relationship

The only moment of doubt occurred when I saw the final papers. The company for which my husband had worked for twenty-five years had indeed gone public during the course of our divorce (but after our negotiations), making my husband a genuinely wealthy man. When I saw how much he was now worth, I was stunned. I turned to my attorney and gasped, "Diana! What should I do?"

She looked at me, smiled flatly, and firmly instructed, "Sign the papers. You have what you need, along with something even more valuable than alimony. You have a good relationship with your ex. That's worth more than all his options put together."

She was right. And, after one last huge sigh, I signed the agreement.

It didn't have to work out that way. If I'd let revenge or greed call the shots, if I'd been unable to let go of my dreams of a certain kind of house and a certain kind of life, I probably would have acted in a way that would have cost me for years. I'd watched as the fallout from angry, unfair settlements ate at both men and women years after they'd divorced.

Getting Divorced from a Civil Union

Kathy Anderson

In August 2002 Kathy Anderson and her female partner had invited their friends and family to Vermont to attend their civil union ceremony, an exchange of vows before a justice of the peace that legally united them as a couple. Although their marriage was not legally valid in their home state of New Jersey, when their relationship ended fourteen months later they felt they couldn't just quietly separate but instead filed for a legal divorce.

In this article, Anderson tells about her experience. She explains why it was important for them to legally dissolve the marriage, even though it wasn't necessary to do so in New Jersey. She also talks about joining a women's divorce support group and discovering that even though she is a lesbian and the other women are straight, they all shared the same need for closure and healing.

The moment of the Big Kaboom, when I knew our relationship was over just 14 months after our Vermont civil union, I knew instinctively that I would not be attending the lesbian support group at the gay and lesbian community center for help. Suddenly I had more in common with the straight married neighbors in our New Jersey town.

A Legal Civil Union

In August 2002 my partner and I had gone to City Hall in Burlington [Vermont], and filled out applications for a civil union license. We pledged traditional vows before a justice of

Kathy Anderson, "My Vermont Civil Union Divorce," *The Advocate* (The National Gay & Lesbian Newsmagazine), September 28, 2004, p. 10.

the peace on the banks of Lake Champlain. At our wedding reception in New Jersey a few months later, our friends and family toasted us and danced to a live band.

This was no lesbian second date, no "pull up the U-Haul." After five years together we had carefully prepared for commitment. We had pre-marriage counseling with our Dignity USA chapter priest. We created wills and powers of attorney. Still, nothing prepared me for what the radical act of marriage felt like; for the wild immensity of the ritual; for how deeply open I felt to the sky, the lake, our future together—now connected I felt to our families in spirit.

Longtime residents of New Jersey, we had chosen a civil union in Vermont as the most legal way to marry at the time, announcing it to loved ones with engraved invitations. So when the Big Kaboom hit, there was no way to minimize it to myself or others, no way to slink away and then months later tell all those people, "Oh, yeah, we broke up."

A Legal Union Requires a Legal Divorce

This was no breakup. This was a divorce.

This was a 10-page separation agreement. This was a docket number on a legal complaint for dissolution. This was me swearing to a judge that I told the truth.

Why bother getting a legal dissolution? After all, it's a tremendous challenge. While Vermont has no residency requirement for getting a civil union, for dissolution it has a one-year residency requirement for at least one party. Couples who are joined in Vermont and later ask their state courts to dissolve their out-of-state union face an uphill battle.

People have asked me kindly, "How legal was it anyway? You live in New Jersey, and your civil union only really counted if you live in Vermont." Talking to a friend, I struggled to put into words why it felt so vital. It wasn't for financial reasons: We had no children, no joint property. "Why, not suing for dissolution would invalidate the whole thing," she said wisely. And that was it, the word I was searching for. I would not invalidate our civil union by agreeing that it didn't count.

Joining a Support Group

Grieving, heartsick, I began dissolution proceedings and joined a women's divorce support group, sponsored by the local chapter of the National Organization for Women, searching for closure and healing. Every week, as new women joined the circle, I had to come out again as a lesbian married in a civil union. When I said my partner was a woman, the only difference I noticed in other women's reactions was a perceptible leaning-in, as if they were hoping for something new, a uniquely lesbian slant on this painful journeys—because the tales told around that table were as predictable as nightfall. But there was nothing unique in my story.

Slowly my divorce group buddies and I healed together; learned that forgiveness saves your life; that taking responsibility for your own part, whether big or small, makes you a divorce survivor, not a victim.

I still believe that marriage will bring most of us incredible blessings. But when our marriages don't work, I hope we insist on proper divorces, with lawyers and judges in our courts, because we deserve to honor our unions with this validation too. We deserve help breaking up households and navigating custody of children. Just as we insist on the right to marry, we have to demand that the legal system help us dissolve our unions when we have to. Because these are not empty ceremonial gestures we are making in Vermont and Massachusetts and Oregon and San Francisco. Our marriages count.

Jewish Divorce

Janis Rapoport

At the invitation of a cousin, Janis Rapoport attended a Jewish divorce ceremony to act as witness to the event. The cousin would receive a Get*, or bill of divorce, from a rabbinical council. Later, a petition would be filed with the authorities to apply for a legal divorce.*

Taking a step back into time, the two women entered the synagogue dressed in long-sleeved blouses and floor-length skirts. Seven men were present to complete the ritual. The Get *document was written by hand by a professionally trained scribe. A rabbi directed the process. Rapoport describes the ceremony as well as some of the ramifications for her cousin. For example, the cousin is expected to not remarry within ninety-two days of the* Get *in order to more easily determine the paternity of any children who might be born to her.*

Shortly before my cousins' 27th wedding anniversary I received an invitation—to attend their divorce.

The event was not scheduled to take place in a legally sanctioned setting, as one might expect. That would come later, after the terms of separation were agreed upon and registered with provincial authorities along with a petition for divorce.

We were going before a *Beit Din*, a house of justice commonly known as a rabbinical court, in order to obtain a *Get*, a letter or bill of divorce sought when the couple is Jewish. This mandate appears in the Bible in Deuteronomy 24:1–3 and in the Talmud, the collected records of generations of academic discussion and judicial administration of Jewish law.

Our roles were predetermined: my female cousin by marriage would receive a ritually prepared document of release

Janis Rapoport, "Jewish Divorce: Intricate and Precise," *Globe & Mail*, July 10, 2003, p. A20.

and I would be her witness. However, I also felt some responsibility for her equanimity during a procedure that comes with a reputation of being traumatic, and hoped she would be treated with respect.

Stepping Into the Past

When we stepped across the threshold of time into the synagogue within whose walls the *Beit Din* had convened, we shifted from the 21st century back to the 17th, or possibly even earlier, and from what I call a technopolis to a Chagall-like European *shtetl* [a small Jewish Eastern European town]. Fortunately, we were both appropriately dressed in long skirts and blouses whose sleeves reached our wrists.

Seven men awaited us in a large book-lined room. My cousin, who appeared somewhat overwhelmed, sat down facing them. The rabbi with whom she had previously met introduced the others. Some wore traditional orthodox black suits and tall hats and had mature beards that appeared never to have been trimmed.

I had to confirm my cousin's identity even after she had shown her driver's licence and other official documents, although my own credentials were neither questioned nor authenticated.

Because my cousin had requested that her husband—my actual blood relation—not be present, his place was taken by a proxy. To divorce with a proxy increases the cost, to (at most) about one-tenth of that for an uncontested civil action. The only cheaper—and simpler—way to download a failed marriage is online, although even then information must be filed in a government court.

The Jewish Divorce Process

Jewish divorce is intricate and precise, delicate and complex. It is the husband who initiates the process. At the *Beit Din* he instructs a professionally trained scribe to prepare the Bill of

Divorce, also known as a *Sefer Keritut*, a scroll of cuffing-off. Under the direction of an ordained rabbi who is specifically trained in the necessary requirements, the scribe inks the requisite 12 lines in Aramaic or Hebrew on a single piece of parchment or vellum, usually with a quill pen. Twelve corresponds to the sum of the Hebrew letters that comprise the word *Get*. *Gimmel* has the numerical value of three and *tet*, nine. With this old-fashioned method there is no need to worry about interference from power outages or computer crashes.

After confirming her voluntary acceptance of the *Get*, my cousin had to cover her head and remove her rings. She stood with open hands, into which the proxy dropped the folded paper. She was then instructed to carry the *Get* about halfway down the room. As she turned to do so, the late morning sunlight shattered into thousands of tiny dots conveyed on the backs of dust-mote banners that unfurled through the windows.

On the other hand it seemed as though the pendulum of progress in women's rights had swung so far forward that it was now oscillating back several centuries where the clockwork of orthodoxy was patiently waiting.

Yet there are Biblical scholars who cite 7,000-year-old *papyri Ketubbot* (Jewish marriage contracts) that provide equally for the termination of a marriage by either husband or wife, a practice that seems to have been abandoned for centuries.

Lastly, the *Ketubah* needed to be nullified. My cousin had been afraid the marriage document that had been written in fine calligraphy and embellished in greens, blues and reds would be ripped or destroyed. However, the rabbi simply marked the *Ketubah* indelibly, to be filed away along with the *Get*.

On receipt of the *p'tur* certificate of proof of release from the marriage, my cousin felt a spontaneous and spiritual lightening. Participating in the *Get* ceremony had also provided whatever deliverance she felt necessary in order to carry on living in a healthy and positive manner.

After the Divorce

My cousin is forbidden to marry a *Kohen*, a member of the priestly caste. Additionally, should she wish to remarry she cannot do so for 92 days, in order to facilitate determination of paternity. This requirement applies even to women past child-bearing age. There is no such restriction for men, by whose laws many Jewish women continue to abide. Such male authority can be rationalized by those who consider the sexes in Judaism are assigned equal but different roles and responsibilities, a position not accepted in more egalitarian communities.

In the contemporary reality of orthodox Jewish divorce, it is still the husband who must agree. If not, and his wife remarries a Jewish man after a civil process, that union is considered adulterous and any children are deemed illegitimate and consequently ineligible to participate in religious rites. A woman who remains undivorced because of her husband's intransigency is considered to be an *agunah* abandoned yet chained. She is not permitted to remarry let alone date anyone.

As we left the *Beit Din*, advancing unnoticed into the 21st century, we walked toward our individual futures across a schoolyard carpeted with myriad dandelions in bright yellow splendour. I suggested we go out for lunch to mark the occasion in a less formal manner. Although you're no longer my cousin by marriage, I said over coffee, you're still my cousin, though now by divorce.

Being Divorced and Catholic

Elsie Radtke

A divorced Catholic herself, Elsie Radtke discusses some of the misconceptions that Catholics have about divorce. She explains that divorced people are allowed to fully participate in the life of the church, including attending Mass, teaching religious education, and receiving the Eucharist (Communion). Participation is only limited if a divorced Catholic remarries without seeking an annulment from the church.

Radtke also talks about the opportunities for spiritual growth presented by divorce, and considers the movement of a divorced person towards new life to be a metaphor for the Resurrection. She looks at her own remarriage and active life in the church and expresses gratitude for the support she has received from the church.

Thirty years ago I walked down the church aisle on my father's arm to be married. The church and reception were filled with well-wishing family and friends. Little did I suspect that 14 years and three children later, we would be divorced. Since that time I have been through the annulment process and am now remarried and a stepmother to three children, yet the shock and stigma of divorce still affects me. I often still wonder how this happened to me.

Most couples enter into marriage with every intention and hope to be together forever. Marriage preparation programs like PreCana give couples a good preview of the skills they will need to achieve a successful marriage. Yet divorce continues to be a traumatic reality in many Catholic families. It rends families apart and leaves everyone wounded and hurting. It destroys trust in children as well as in adults. It takes

Elsie Radtke, "Not Divorced From My Faith," *U.S. Catholic*, vol. 71, July 2006, p. 50.

years to recover from divorce, and it leaves a void that can only be accepted, never filled.

I had a very difficult time with my divorce. I had been taught that good Catholics do not divorce. I believed that if you kept the rules, attended church, and lived a life of faith, you'd be rewarded with a successful marriage, good children, etc. My parents had been married more than 40 years. They had disagreements, but they worked things out. When I ran out of tactics to save my marriage, I felt lost and abandoned.

Years later I heard a priest equate the pain of divorce with the pain Jesus must have experienced in the Garden of Gethsemane. Hearing that, I felt that God understood the isolation, alienation, and profound sadness I was feeling. Jesus must have felt similarly when his people turned their backs on him.

Divorced Catholics Often Feel Judged

Catholics who are divorced often feel judged by their fellow Catholics. And misconceptions abound. At divorce support groups, attendees often share their sadness that once they were divorced, they were told they could no longer be eucharistic ministers. I have received phone calls from teachers who feared being removed from their positions in Catholic schools because they were going through a divorce. Protestant churches are populated with many divorced Catholics who have given up on their own church.

I know a woman who had not been to church in 13 years because "someone" at her church had told her that she was excommunicated because of her divorce. She longed to receive the Eucharist and cried when she told me she was afraid that she "would die and go to hell." She had been married to an alcoholic and drug addict.

Divorced People Can Still Be Active Catholics

The truth is that since the Second Vatican Council Catholics who are divorced have complete access to life in the church.

They may participate at Mass, receive the Eucharist, teach religious education, be eucharistic ministers, lectors, and ushers at their church. It is only when divorced Catholics remarry without seeking and receiving an annulment that they are restricted in participation.

A while after my divorce, I was at Mass with my three children. During the Prayers of the Faithful, the deacon asked us to pray for "families and children suffering the pain of divorce." The congregation responded, "Lord, hear our prayer." When my kids heard this petition and response, they sat up straight, looked at me, and said, "Mom, I think they're praying for us." They loved it.

Divorce can be an opportunity for growth, self-knowledge, and rich spiritual understanding of what it means to be Catholic. Divorced Catholics make great contributions to the Catholic community. The richness of their faith and the insight they have into the Resurrection can be used to influence marriage preparation programs and extend compassionate outreach throughout all of the church's ministries. Their embrace of a new dream and a new life shows the entire community that resurrection is not just a promise for our bodies but a reality for our lives right now.

Although I would not have thought this possible a few years ago, I have found happiness in a loving marriage and a rewarding career in family ministry in my church. I have again found much to be thankful for. Let's make sure other divorced people can feel the support of the church, too.

Chapter 3

Moving On

Becoming a Single Father

Michael Evangelista

Michael Evangelista was in a traditional marriage in which his wife took care of the bulk of the child-rearing duties. He considered himself to be a devoted father but trusted his wife to take care of the day-to-day details. When their third child was still an infant, Evangelista's wife suddenly began to withdraw from the family. He soon found himself in the position of single father, first with two of their children living with him, then with all three.

In this article, he talks about the challenges he has faced and lessons he has learned. Although consumed by feelings of pain and grief, he realized that the children needed him to believe in himself, to assure them they would all be fine. Eventually, he noticed that that was indeed the case. He has learned from the children and from those around him that after facing many and frequent mistakes, sufferings, and defeats, he is able to begin again, over and over.

I cannot think in straight lines anymore. Plans, worries, even spoken sentences come in broken waves. Focusing on a single task without being interrupted? Impossible. I am a madman. I am half asleep. I am a single father.

I've had to learn to see double, keeping the big ball rolling while juggling a full complement of sidetracks and minor emergencies. School days are the most hectic, and today is no exception. I'm pulling my boots on, packing lunches, eating a quick breakfast, and jotting down scrambled thoughts from last night's foggy dreaming. Tuesday morning, just as usual.

It hasn't always been this way. I was a devoted dad from the start, but I didn't always pay so much attention to every detail of the children's lives. Their mother and I had taken on surprisingly traditional roles: If I provided food, shelter, and an occasional hand with the basic chores, she seemed content to devote her days entirely to their care. And I was secure in knowing that someone was there for them when I could not be.

From homebirths to cloth diapers, homeschool to home-cooked meals, she was not just a mother but the mother. She birthed and nursed three healthy babies as if it were all she knew. It was not without its struggles and pain, but we were a team and we were going somewhere, rewriting the scripts of our lives one chapter at a time.

His Wife Suddenly Shut Down

And then, suddenly, after the third child was weaned—the third and final act somehow in her mind, now complete—the lights went down, and a dark, heavy curtain closed behind her eyes. All we saw of her after that was a fleeting glimpse as she slipped through the stage-left door, abandoning her once-fulfilling role as the ultimate natural mother for some other life. She seemed to vanish almost overnight, leaving costumes and props scattered about the stage. Meanwhile, the children and I sat alone in the front row of an empty theater, wondering where to go.

What else could we do but button up our coats against the cold and darkness and move on? We cleaned up the mess, packed up the few belongings that were not sold or given away, and headed out west—to Utah, to Grandma, and to a new beginning.

Moving to Utah with Two Children, Leaving One Behind

In the haste and confusion of post-divorce compromise, it seemed best that the youngest child, at the time just two years old, stay in Florida with his mother. She acted as if it were some great, final decision, a permanent way to justify the loss of the other two; for me, it was a desperate sacrifice, in order to gain a little time and speed in getting reestablished on a new frontier.

I spent my days in prayer for him and my nights in tears. I would never suggest that any couple separate their kids, yet even now I'm not sure I could have made that cross-country trip with all three of my children. Letting Ezra stay behind was, by far, the hardest thing I have ever done, but somehow I knew—perhaps because of the ease with which their mother surrendered the other two—that it would not be long before my kids were all reunited. Indeed, within a couple of months, the youngest came to join us.

Learning to Believe in Himself

I might have stayed closer and tried to work with her, sharing the kids, swapping schedules. But after many attempts to pacify her ever-changing demands and intentions, it was clear that we could never work out a serious long-term plan. I prayed, worried, and stewed for so long, and then, finally, a voice began to speak up inside of me: "It's okay to believe in yourself. The children need you to be happy."

I want to be able to say, as so many single mothers have told me, that I knew we would be fine, that the children were my life, my joy, all I'd ever need. If the kids remember that time at all, I'm sure they would see me as full of strength, love, and courage. I had to be, for them. But in truth, I have never been so scared and unsure of the future as I was then. My only guidance was that small inner voice. And, as in all of the deepest times in my life, I understood that inner guidance is all I ever really have, sink or swim.

The first stage, of stone-cold grieving, was so consuming, and the second phase—keeping everything up and running once I'd stopped moping—was so demanding, that it seems only recently that I've been able to pause and look around.

There was one day, just a few weeks ago, when I realized that I am actually making it work. It's like learning to ride a bicycle and finally getting the courage to look behind you, only to see that the person you thought was holding you upright let go a hundred yards back. "I'm really doing it." I said to no one but myself, and felt the burden get just a little bit lighter.

I have learned much about life and myself in a very short time. Introspection and analysis have certainly brought some insights, but nothing has taught me more than pain. The world as I had known it turned upside down, and all of my hopes, fears, and understanding ended up in a cluttered pile. At times, in anger, I have tried to reduce the mess of my life, to simplify and finalize the process in one fast cut. And each time I have been shown it's just not that simple, and that the process is a long way from any final place of understanding.

Reminded by the Children

One such attempt at closure was particularly humbling. I came home from work in a rage, determined to make a change. I had spent six painful months trying to make sense of an experience that seemed entirely senseless. Now I decided it was time to clean house. With dirt on my hands and wet mud still clinging to my boots, I flew in the front door and began tearing through kitchen cabinets, closets, and dresser drawers, determined to throw away or destroy anything that reminded me of her. The shirt from my 21st birthday, the leather coat that had been her brother's—even our worn-out toaster-oven, a wedding gift—all of it had to go. I was starting clean, determined to make my own memories from now on.

I filled two boxes and was standing atop the washing machine, tossing things from the pantry shelves over my shoulder into a third box, when two small voices spoke up behind me. "Whatcha doin'?" "When's dinner?"

I turned to answer the children, at the time just four and five years old, but the words failed to come. In an instant, my balloon of self-empowerment and decisive anger was burst by the tiniest of pins. I cannot know whether I was laughing or crying as I realized what I should have seen all along: I would never be truly free of the past. Its memories were here, flesh and blood, pleading in small, sincere voices for my attention. I could toss out the gifts, but I would never be without my kids.

On that day, I took one small step toward making peace with the past, realizing that scars and bad memories are not all that it has given me. Being solely responsible for three children is an incredible burden, but it's also my motivation and my direction. My relationship to them is the axis around which all of my life revolves. As in any relationship, we have our good times and our bad. Sometimes I get afraid or worn down, and I yell a little louder than I should. Other times, when I'm feeling lost and in the dark, it is the kids' love and patience that bring me back to real life, to the moment.

Growth and Survival

It is certainly true that children are resilient beings, and these kids have bounced back incredible. So many things seem to have rolled right off them. As a child of divorced parents, I've spent many hours being afraid for my own children and the pain that I know they will carry their whole lives. Though I tell myself that I am not to blame, I have felt my share of guilt over letting them suffer. But there is a flaw in this emotion, for often it is the guilt itself that hurts them. It weighs so heavily on me that I am less than my best for them. I have learned that my kids don't expect me to be sorry or perfect; they just want me to be myself and to love them. I continue to stumble, and they continue to wait, smiling, for me to stand again. I know that I am the grow-up, but I realized long ago that they are also raising me.

Now that I have all three of the children with me, it seems logical that I should be able to simply remove the faulty wiring and make a nice, smooth reentry into normal life. Contrary to all of my rational, male instincts, however, I have had to accept that logic is powerless against the raw, hard force of emotional disaster. Rather than smashing down the past, I must learn to carry it, accept it, and build upon the rocky foundation of my early life. This is more than living; it is growth and survival.

The best thoughts, it seems, come during the times when I can embrace the entire drama of my life—the pain, the fear, the endless and demanding work, the memories. All of these are moving to form me, to shape my growth. This is my life, and every moment, good or bad, is a piece of who I am and who I will become.

A Lesson from a Friend with Cancer

My good friend Thomas was losing his body to systemic cancer. The last time I saw him, I was at the peak of my divorce and emotional distress; I could not eat, rarely slept, and had taken up smoking and self-pity as full-time habits. And here was my friend, a husband and father, chronically coughing, painfully slipping over to the other side. Yet Thomas refused to frown or feel sorry for himself or for me. He had seen the true beauty that is beyond all our agony, and he knew that sometimes the hardest parts are the most important.

Despite his own pain, Tom looked at me with utter compassion. He held his arms in close like a cradle and said, in a voice that wanted only to rest, "When I am angry, I rock my anger like a baby. I hold it and I nurture it, and after a while, it stops crying."

Of all the talking, listening, thinking, and explaining I have done in this past year, no words have been nearly as relevant or as humbling as these. When I can hold the suffering and sadness in my heart, and look with eyes that continue to see beauty, it is then that I truly am alive.

Each day there are a hundred mistakes and a thousand chances to do better. Life has become a series of challenges, triumphs, and defeats. My heart is often heavy, but my mind knows that I am free to begin, over and over, to make the best of what I have been given. Some nights, all I can do is crash and burn; but in the morning, like some mythical bird, I arise out of the ashes for another try at flying.

The Confusing Role of Ex-Stepfather

William Jelani Cobb

In this article, William Jelani Cobb considers the confusing role he finds himself in as an ex-stepfather. Cobb had been dating Shana, Aiesha's mother, since Aiesha was two years old. Aiesha's biological father did not play a role in her life, so when Cobb married Shana he took on the role of father. Later, after a divorce, he still feels like a father but misses being part of Aiesha's daily life. He muses about how the relationship may be changed in the future—by Shana meeting someone else who takes on the role of father, by a career move that separates them geographically, or just by the passing of time—and wonders how long he can continue to act as Aiesha's father.

I wake up each morning and think about Aiesha, first thing. I haven't spoken to her in a month, but all her messages are still saved on my answering machine. There is a T-shirt in the exact spot she left it on her last visit three months ago. I still tell her that she is my favorite person. Aiesha is 8, spoiling for 9. She is my daughter, once removed.

In my wide-eyed youth I subscribed to such naive notions as love makes one a parent, and "23 chromosomes don't make you Daddy." I believed that fatherhood is created every morning at 6:00 A.M., when you creak out of bed to crack eggs, rattle pans and let yourself be hustled into granting your kid ten more minutes of sleep. I still believe that genes don't make the parent, but now I ask, what does a voided wedding vow make me?

If you listen to the running dialogue on talk radio, in barbershops and from pulpits, the American father has been dispatched, part of some planned obsolescence, done in by feminism and sperm banks. The old Dad model has been discontinued in favor of a newer, sleeker, single-parent alternative. I don't subscribe to that theory, but I do think we're in danger of becoming a society of temporary families. We're full of books and how-to guides that make it easier for people to survive the end of a marriage, but as a consequence, we run the risk of making divorce a cure-all for marital woe.

Becoming a Father

I know Aiesha because her mother, Shana, was my college girlfriend, and I broke up with her and then years later found myself wishing for her again. She was wild and beautiful, the opposite of my self-conscious, bookish ways. We were done in less than six months but stayed in touch with each other. Five years later I moved to New York for graduate school. When we threw a surprise party for my mother's fiftieth birthday, I invited Shana, and she showed up with a buoyant 2-year-old who had impossibly round cheeks and whose favorite word was no! As in "You are adorable." "No!"

Soon Shana and I were hanging out again, back to our old routines. When I occasionally spent the night, I slept on the couch so that Aiesha wouldn't get the wrong idea. The first night we slept together again, Shana told me that she wasn't looking for another short-term relationship. I understood; neither was I. At some point in those first months of being reunited, I realized that I loved Shana again and that Aiesha had already chosen me as her father. Shana and I got married.

I think men secretly want to raise their daughters to be the kind of women who were out of their league when they were young. And so it was with Aiesha. But really, it was about the words, teaching her the words to old classics like "Ain't No Sunshine" and giggling through the part where Bill Withers sings, "And I know, I know, I know, I know, I know. . ." Kids dig repetition. She turned out volumes of poems, plays, songs and stories that were duly typed up and E-mailed to all my friends, coworkers and distant relatives as evidence of her burgeoning literary genius.

The Marriage Fell Apart

There were signs early on, now that I think of it, that the marriage was headed south. I saw in gradual degrees that my wife was less and less interested in our relationship and knew that I was at the point where many a man would've bailed. I chose to work harder. When the newspapers ranked Aiesha's public school in the bottom half of those in the city, I reduced my grad classes and worked part-time to send her to a private school. When Shana was stuck at work a few hours before her women's-group meeting was to be held in our apartment, I came home early and surprised her by cleaning up and preparing the food. I was like an outfielder who knows that the ball is headed for the bleachers, but smashes face first into the wall trying to catch it anyway. In my world, there was no such thing as a warning track.

A marital cliche: You're in the kitchen cooking dinner when your spouse returns home from a hard day at the office and announces that it's over. Just like that. It's a scenario that any writing instructor worth his salt would trash, but that's really how it went down. The exact words: "I don't love you the way a wife should love a husband, and I would like you to move out." Then silence. I was broken for a long time afterward. Shana had married me because I was the proverbial good catch, not out of a desire to build a lifelong connection. When Shana asked me to leave, I stared at her blankly for about five minutes. When she told Aiesha that I was leaving, Aiesha asked, "Does this mean I don't have a father anymore?"

Being An Ex-Stepfather

There are easy answers. Friends (mainly female) tell me once a father, always a father. But experience tells me differently—that I could just as easily be evicted again, that Shana could remarry and leave me a parental second-string player. Experience has taught me that ex-stepfather does not exist as a census category. That I no longer qualify for a Father's Day card.

Looking at it now, I know that I deeply and profoundly love that little girl. I understand the weight of the bond between parent and child. I also know that I was trying to single-handedly undo the mythology directed at Black men, that I wanted a family that would laugh past the bleak statistics and damning indictments of Black male irresponsibility. When I married Shana, Aiesha had not seen her biological father in more than a year. As far as I know, she has not seen him since. I saw tragedy in her growing up as yet another fatherless Black girl, another child whose father abandoned her in favor of emptier pursuits. I wanted to be like my old man, quietly heroic in raising my brother and sister and never once letting on that they were not his biological kin. I wanted to be a keeper.

An Undefined Relationship

These days, I know that my relationship with Aeisha is unwieldy, that it is sagging under the weight of its own ambiguity. Fatherhood is all about watching the daily changes, the new word learned or noticing that now she doesn't have to stand on a stool to reach her toothbrush. But I know that in a year or two my work may require that I move to Texas or California or Alaska, and it's possible that I'll fade from her preadolescent memory.

Christmas is a hard, bright day, and I wake up alone with my head heavy from the previous night's bender. Aiesha has left me a message saying that she has a gift for me and could I please come today so she can give it to me. Her mother and I have lived apart for six months, and I don't know Aiesha as well as I did in June. In another six months, she'll be a different child altogether.

When I see her outside, riding her bike in the parking lot of her building, I think how she has grown tall and slender as a reed. I bought her a watch, yellow and red, but with no cartoon characters because Aiesha fancies herself a sophisticate. The note says, "Dear Aiesha: My father once told me that keeping track of time is the first step to becoming an adult. I hope you think of me when you wear this." She gives me a gift card, and written in her best 8-year-old scrawl it says simply, "I love you." She's telling me the plot points to her latest story, the one she wants to publish when she's 12. A moment later she wants me to toss her into the air and pleads "one more time" until my deltoids are burning. She still remembers most of the words to "Ain't No Sunshine." Today, she's my daughter. Today.

Beginning a New Life

Margie Kaplan

In this essay, Margie Kaplan talks about the circumstances of her divorce and then begins to outline, year by year, the stages she went through while recovering. She describes the first year as numb. *She attempted to keep life as unaltered as possible for the sake of her two children. By the second year, she had passed through the time of pure survival mode and was ready to experience the feeling of sadness. In the third year, she got past her fear of not being as physically attractive as she once had been and began dating again. In subsequent years, she has become much more the creator of her own destiny, making her own choices and choreographing her life into what she calls "My Own Dance."*

In June 1992 [my husband] Ted had raised the issue of our separating, and I panicked and got us into couples' counseling and tried to be perfect in the ways I thought he wanted me to be. We were like cement blocks sleeping together over those months. The tension was so thick. All I knew then was that he wanted to leave *me*. He was staying because of the agreement, but not really present in any way, so that night in September as he tyrannically towered over me, with his lifetime of rage focused, laserlike, down on me, I broke through the fear of rejection that had been with me since my father died when I was six and said "GET THE F--- OUT NOW."

Beginning a New Life

This was the beginning of a new life. I think I actually felt better, though terrified about working out the arrangements,

Margie Kaplan, *Cut Loose: (Mostly) Older Women Talk about the End of (Mostly) Long-Term Relationships, Piscataway*. NJ: Rutgers University Press, 2006.

telling the kids, et cetera. How were we going to do this? Ted went out and got a sublet and we planned the family discussion.

Telling the Children

The kids were nine and five that fall. I was forty-seven. We gathered in the living room for a family meeting and explained (I think mainly Ted), that we hadn't been getting along and that Daddy was going to move out and get another place. Our oldest immediately began wailing, crouched in the corner of our living room. We explained that they had nothing to do with this, we loved them dearly, we would both always be their parents, yada, yada, yada. We did it "the right way."

Though I don't think our youngest got it. When she saw her sister sobbing, she too began crying and asking questions. Only now do I realize the amazing similarity to what I experienced as the youngest child in 1952, at age six, sitting with my family of two sisters in a car as my mother explained to us that Poppy, our father, had "gone away on a long trip" (talk about euphemisms). My oldest sister began crying and I, like *my* youngest, lacking the cognitive development, but astute in emotions, joined in the sob fest. Words were irrelevant. Tragedy was present.

As painful as that grueling evening was, I felt the tension lifted, and though life was heavy, it was beginning anew instead of being a day-to-day experience in anxiety and fear. This was true for my kids as well. Words need not be spoken for dissension and anger to permeate an environment. This was finally over and we moved on.

Ted took the kids to see his/their new place and he and I "lawyered up" for the nightmare of the next year of sorting out our arrangements. He left in late September never to return overnight again.

Year One: Numb

I would describe year one as *numb*. My job as I saw it was to keep my kids' lives as unaltered as possible—in practical ways, obviously. Luckily I had a wonderful circle of friends who supported me and dished Ted. Several said they felt this was going to be great for me as I had become eclipsed, even with my big personality, by his life and needs. These friends made a big difference.

I began a push to increase my practice which I had let dwindle as PTA and Brownie troop had absorbed my time. I knew I was going to need money. That's what our two lady lawyers haggled over. It took one year for us to resolve a separation agreement, which later became incorporated into our divorce. To comment simply on that, Ted felt he paid too much and I felt not enough, so it is probably a somewhat appropriate settlement plan. His income was more than twice mine at that time.

There was no disagreement about the kids. They were living with me and Ted had dinners twice weekly and overnight visits to his apartment every other weekend. I think this was more than enough for him at the time. I will never forget that first weekend at Daddy's. He got the kids at about ten on a Saturday morning. I wandered around the apartment from room to room crying, feeling so forlorn. With the exception of a professional conference or something scheduled well ahead for Ted to take care of the kids, I had not had a day alone, to say nothing of an overnight, for years. I will admit it didn't take long for me to savor the new experience.

The year passed, I worked at my practice, I began teaching at a college, I oversaw my kids' activities and care and food and home love. They were/are my family and they were the biggest support I had. I was nose to the grindstone with all I had to do—numb, not sad, not angry, just pushing forward. I don't remember thinking about romance, sex, partnering, et cetera. This meant I was alien even to myself.

Things went generally well. The kids continued to seem happy, doing well in school, having friends, parties, normal life. Ted and I did "together" well in those days—parent-teacher conferences, birthday parties, school productions, et cetera. Our kids had two parents who loved them and were there for them.

I didn't know what Ted was involved in and I believed it wasn't another woman, as he had asserted that while telling me how he hated me that evening months before. So I was quite shaken about three or for months after he moved out when I ran into a well-known entertainer at Barnes and Noble. She had sung some of Ted's work in her cabaret performance and had rehearsed quite a bit at our apartment. She expressed how upset she was at hearing about our breakup and "Was Ted still so smitten with that young, blond ingenue?" I mumbled that I didn't know and got away from her feeling struck. I'm not sure if it was knowing that he left *because* of another woman or if I couldn't bear that I didn't know. I was out of the loop. This is an aspect of life that has been hard for me to accept. Then, it couldn't be OK that I didn't know it all. It's still not a pleasant feeling for me to be outside of the "secret," but now my substance is solid enough to understand and let it be. It also explained the frequent schedule changes Ted made regarding his time with the girls and probably his interest in more stylish dress and presentation. Whatever, she dumped him shortly thereafter and he became the single man-about-town.

Year Two: Sad

Year two was the year of sad. We'd survived and it seemed we'd continue surviving, so I could let go a little and feel, and sad was what was there. Even though I'd been a divorcée at age twenty, my marriage to Ted was what I'd grown up believing life was to be about, raising our children, growing old together, and sharing a life on off into the sunset. I teach the marriage statistics in my psych courses so I am aware that a large 41 percent do not succeed, but I'd not contemplated that on any emotional level. The reality that my life to come had no preexisting fantasy to guide it forward was startling and painful. I was a failure at the way it was supposed to be. I was sad, but scared too.

I cried a lot that year and remembered all the wonderful times Ted and I had shared and felt somewhat desperate about myself and "my failure." I was doomed to be dumped and alone. First Poppy and now Ted. I was not lovable—too many hard edges. I got back into therapy and bemoaned my plight for a while.

Year Three: Back to Dating

Year three, approaching fifty and hadn't had sex since Ted's departure. Obviously I was coming out of my morass. Thinking about sex and closeness is always a healthy sign. Being back out there physically was scary as my naked presentation, two C-sections and a gall bladder removal later, wasn't as secure as when I'd been a tight thirty-five-year-old, but I was determined basically to live on, and this was part of it.

The first icebreaker was not anyone I was interested in. He was a secure test balloon for me and a good reentry. I remember telling myself I *had* to be OK as is. I would not cover up or turn out the lights to protect myself, and walking away from the bed, headed for the bathroom, backside out there in the light after we'd "done the deed," was a noteworthy character builder. I'd be OK. That intimate aspect of my life has been too. I'm lucky and grateful and I work hard at it. I think all three play a part.

Time Passes

The years have continued on, ten more to be exact. The kids have grown. The kids *are* grown and again they're good too. Ted, though always a caring, if distracted, father, went on and continues to be a wannabe lyricist, disgruntled (as the girls tell me) with his work. He has remarried and we have very little to do with each other now. In all these years he has never admitted that we shared many loving, wonderful times together. Last year our youngest sang in a concert. I had given her money to get the lowest-priced tickets for myself, a friend, and my mother. Those seats were sold out so she used a credit card of her dad's to get the next-lowest-priced tickets. I had the extra money in an envelope for him at the concert. My daughter saw him first in the crowd after the performance. I saw him say something into her ear as she came over to us for hugs and accolades about the concert. The first thing she said was "Do you have the money for Dad?" I pulled out the envelope and handed it to her, feeling the raw chill of his disdain. I have never owed him fifty cents over all these years! I don't need to share those earlier memories anymore. I genuinely believe it's his loss.

I still do not ([at] age fifty-eight) have any set future fantasy to strive toward. I've got lots of ideas and each day moves me more toward one, or creates a new possibility. I see life in blocks of time and activities now, not the "young and then married forever" scenario. It continues to be sometimes sad, sometimes scary, but also exciting. I feel much more the creator of my destiny and I know me so much more intimately than I did as Ted's wife, the choreographer for his dance. This life is *my* dance and getting dumped was one of the basic exercises that has built up my strength in creating life, growth, and loving.

Making the Best of Moving On

Carla Sue Nelson

Carla Sue Nelson is a Christian woman starting over after a divorce. In this essay, she looks with a sense of humor at some of the ironies involved in beginning again. She talks about some of the difficult decisions, such as finding a job and selecting a day-care provider, that had to be made at a time when she was in no emotional shape to be making them. She gives some advice about spending money and keeping "shopping therapy" to a minimum. And she looks to her children to help her to laugh and to find the bright side of the situation.

I'm looking in the mirror and thinking to myself, *How in the world am I going to pull this off—a job interview after years of diaper duty and* Teletubbies? On the outside I looked pretty darn good, if I do say so myself. By this time, I was down more than sixty pounds and wearing a svelte size ten. For you "Skinny Minnies" this isn't a big deal, but for us southern gals raised on fried chicken and biscuits, this is monumental. I don't think I even wore a size ten when I was ten! I had on my new powder-blue suit, my power hairdo, and I was ready to take on the world, right? Wrong! On the inside, I was a quivering little child who just wanted to go back to bed and pretend that "this" was happening to someone else.

Important Decisions

Life after divorce is so ironic. You have to make some of the most important decisions in your life—legal, financial, personal, career—when emotionally you really aren't capable of

Carla Sue Nelson, *Live, Laugh, Love Again: A Christian Woman's Guide to Surviving Divorce*. New York: Warner Faith, 2006.

deciding "paper or plastic" at the grocery store. Here I was going for a job interview where you have to "sell yourself" and be confident when I felt like the biggest loser in the world. Don't get me wrong, I was no stranger to hard work, and I knew I had a good résumé and skills, but I was a nervous wreck and pretty much broke out in hives at my prospects. I had held a job since my paper route at age fourteen, but this time it was different. The "plan" had always been for me to be the breadwinner while my husband got his flight hours, and then I would stay at home with the babies until they went to school. I was even going to transition from a marketing career to a teaching career at that time. *Daycare* was practically a four-letter word in our house. Now I had to get a job, find suitable daycare, and get ready to move out of the house within six weeks.

If you are going back to work, I highly recommend a job that doesn't take a lot of brain power and a boss who understands you might be missing some time due to court appearances, real estate matters, insurance, children adjusting to daycare issues, afternoon crying sessions, and chocolate binges. Oh, and don't forget about tax time. I had never been audited in my life, but there must be someone at the IRS [International Revenue Service] who flags the "divorce" returns and decides that the woman just hasn't been through enough, so let's question her return. It was priceless, absolutely priceless. (For the record, I did "win" and received my money with interest. I praise God for my CPA [certified public accountant] and his staff. It was money well-spent.)

Money Issues

Speaking of spending money—don't. Really, this is no time for shopping therapy (or only the minimum level of shopping therapy). I found myself using credit cards like there was no tomorrow. Miss "Debt-Free Living" and Dave Ramsey-wannabe was "Discovering" and "Mastering" all kinds of pretty things. Visa was everywhere I wanted to be. My rationale was that when I moved out, I couldn't bear to take things that held so many memories. I'm telling you now, take it. Paint it if you have to, decoupage it, sell it, whatever. Those things are expensive and difficult to replace.

I also spent out of guilt, trying to replace the "things" my babies had at their "old house" and keep up with Disneyland Dad. Seriously, women use that term to describe an ex-husband who spoils the kids out of guilt for the divorce, but my husband actually took them to Disney World.

Male Attention

Life after divorce is a time of such vulnerability. From the "older" gentleman who just wants to "be there for you" and sends you cuddly teddy bears and cards about how God will take care of you to the young whippersnapper who propositions you in the Sam's Club parking lot, you may get a lot of unwanted attention that is uncomfortable to deal with. I ended up buying a wedding band just to wear and fend off prospective suitors. I'm not saying it wasn't a little bit nice having the attention, especially since I had been with the same man for all of my adult life; but please know that I agree with my fellow authors: when you are newly divorced, this is not a time to start any type of romantic relationship. I made mistakes in this area as I tried to recapture the security and love I had lost. I was naïve and gullible, and I still regret some pretty stupid decisions I made during this time. Thankfully, we have a God of grace and mercy and a Savior whose blood washes away all of the bad stuff. And once your slate is clean, and you have a sense of the new "you" and what you want out of life, then you will be more adept at dating.

One of my favorite memories of "life after divorce" was when my children and I were sitting in our little apartment eating dinner and trying to ignore some noisy teenagers outside our window. I told my precious toddlers that one day

God would bring a wonderful man into Mommy's life who would love her and be a wonderful stepdaddy and go to church with us. My four-year-old son pondered this for a while and then said, "What about the Domino's Pizza guy." I began to laugh hysterically as I thought about it from his point of view. All you had to do was call, he came running, and he brought steaming hot pepperoni pizza. Of course he was the perfect guy for Mommy!

Take Time to Laugh

That laugh was very therapeutic. Find the bright side of things, and try to laugh a lot. It's certainly better than all that crying!

After divorce, as in all of life, there are highs and lows. One minute you're facing the fact that you really should be tested for sexually transmitted diseases if your husband had other partners. The next minute you're at the park blowing bubbles and laughing with your kids because now you know how very precious every moment with them really is. The bad stuff you've been through really has a way of illuminating the good. So focus on the good stuff as much as you can, and give the bad stuff to God.

Blending Two Families in Remarriage

Wendy Swallow

A number of years went by after Wendy Swallow's divorce before she decided to remarry. Her two boys were in their teens. Her new husband, Charlie, also had two teenage boys and together they became a blended family. She discusses some of their challenges and triumphs in this excerpt from her book, The Triumph of Love over Experience.

Knowing that many remarried couples get divorced again in the first few years, Swallow and her husband made a commitment to stay married for at least five years, instead of dissolving the relationship the first time it became difficult. They worked hard at keeping a balance between their relationship with each other and their relationships with their children. They tried to find activities that the whole family could participate in, but each parent also spent time with his or her own children. Swallow also talks in general about the characteristics of a blended family, using her family as an example.

One of the most challenging tasks for remarried couples is establishing what kind of family you will be, and we struggled with that mightily. What do you do when one person doesn't like skiing or someone else can't stand cats? Do you enjoy political debates at the dinner table or stay up late watching basketball? What do you allow and what do you restrict? Each bold stroke calls for compromise, for individual sacrifices, for everyone to learn to share and take turns and bend. Stepfamily experts call this investing in the we that is the core of a successful remarriage. [My husband] Charlie and I work harder to create this we than the kids do, but they have been

Wendy Swallow, *The Triumph of Love over Experience: A Memoir of Remarriage*. New York: Hyperion, 2004.

coming along. I put pictures of our vacations into collages and hang them on the walls, to remind us of the family unit that will be the bedrock of our future together. Charlie organizes trips that everybody will enjoy—even the guy who isn't wild about skiing. If we're trying to pull off a special surprise for one of them, we get everybody in on the ruse.

Over time, our biological boundaries have started to soften, though I would hardly say we are a blended family or that we look anything like a traditional nuclear family. Charlie and his sons sometimes go on trips without the rest of us; sometimes we go visit my parents without them. Other times, we all go together. Sometimes I think we should push for more togetherness, but then reality hits me in the face. Their sports and activity schedules are so demanding, there is no way one parent could tend to all of them with anything like the level of attention our kids get from the two of us operating our own subfamily units. It's taken several years for me to absorb the history on my stepsons—their emotional challenges, academic ups and downs—and I still don't know the half of it. It's a challenge to feel like a family when you don't even know each other that well.

Kids Get to Know Each Other

Truth be told, our kids were less than enthusiastic about living with each other. They didn't necessarily like each other and they were worried about losing their privileges and parental attention. In the beginning, this worried me more than anything. In those early months I watched their interactions like a playground monitor: ready to leap in and break it up if things got dicey. But after a while I relaxed. They have too much respect for their parents and too little personal agony to really go after each other. They circled for several years, not sure they liked their new relatives, but now are closing in slowly, as teenage boys will do, connecting as much as they can without embarrassing themselves. Every Christmas they buy each other more presents, because they know each other better. They tease, they compete, they challenge each other with math problems over the dinner table. They are boys, after all. Sometimes they advise each other, talk about colleges, encourage each other, and offer help. I know they will never feel like blood brothers, but I hope that as they grow older they will seek one another out more, enjoy one another's company at family events, rely on one another as Charlie and I age. I hope their children will feel like cousins.

Promise to Stay Married Five Years

When Charlie and I married, we made a deal: no matter how hard it got, we wouldn't divorce for five years. By then most of the kids would be off to college, and we figured we would have a chance to renew our relationship if it had weakened under the stress of raising the four boys. I had read the harrowing statistics on remarriage failure and was determined to outlast them, if nothing else.

When a remarried couple can't hold it together, the familiar disintegration often happens shockingly fast. Unlike first marriages, which usually enjoy several years of romantic bliss before problems start to emerge, study after study confirms that the majority of remarriages, particularly those with kids, will struggle through the first two to five years, as everyone fights to adapt to the new family, new territory, new rules, and new family culture. Unfortunately, about half of those will not make it through that testing period. Once people decide it isn't working, they tend to move out quickly—sometimes, the therapists say, before they've even tried to make things better.

Divided Loyalties

What goes wrong when remarriages fail? Is it always about the kids, the enduring reality that blood is thicker than water and that loyalty questions will always result in a balkanized household—mother with her kids on one side, dad with his kids on the other? In the course of trying to negotiate the new marriage, a day inevitably comes when one partner turns to the other, in a moment of pain and disbelief, and says, "Are you asking me to choose between you and my kids?"

This is the most harrowing of questions, because it reveals the very core of what drives second marriages apart. But I believe that the question itself—and the tendency to see things as a struggle between the marriage and one's children—is the problem, not the answer. When this moment came in the second winter of my remarriage, over some question about discipline, I instinctively backed down. I was mad as hell at that moment, but I could still see the big warning sign flashing in my head.

"No," I replied, "I will never ask you to make that choice." I knew in my heart that I would only lose. So I backed up, asked myself some hard questions about my own contribution to the problem, and let go of my resentment. When I had calmed down, I went back to Charlie with some ideas and solutions, rather than ultimatums.

Keep Trying New Things

What I'm learning is that the path to a resolution is never straight for us. We meander, try new things, go back, get help, look at maps, dig tunnels. Sometimes we get there faster than other times. I'm learning to trust the process and count forward motion of any sort as a blessing. For someone who has always been results oriented, this Zenlike approach to life is not easy. In fact it is often frustrating, but in time I think we will find our way through the maze and discover that we have built support for each other in the process.

Ironically, the experts say it isn't necessarily the loyalty problems and fights that doom a remarriage as much as how people fight and whether they can ultimately resolve their problems. Psychologist E. Mavis Hetherington says she was surprised to find that frequent fighting was not a good predictor of remarital breakup—it was more how people fought. In her study she found that high levels of contempt, hostile criticism, and withdrawal were the most clear predictors of marital breakup whether in a first marriage or remarriage.

Problem Behaviors

Psychologist John M. Gottman of the University of Washington has done fascinating studies of interpersonal behavior between married people, and found that he can predict which couples are headed for divorce by the degree to which they display what he calls marriage's Four Horsemen of the Apocalypse: hostile criticism, contempt, denial, and withdrawal. Couples who indulge in this kind of disdain and rigidity need help, and need it fast.

These qualities feel familiar, because I saw them emerge in my first marriage. I know how corrosive contempt can be in an intimate relationship. I know that there are points past which a marriage cannot recover. What Gottman has discovered is that our marital interactions—in fact, all our social interactions—are composed of hundreds of emotional bids for connection between people. "These bids can be a question, a look, an affectionate touch on the arm, or any single expression that says 'I want to feel connected to you,'" Gottman says. Those bids, and whether they get a negative or a positive response, create the fabric of a relationship. We know when we are ignoring or dissing [disrespecting] someone, as my children would put it—and we do it at our peril.

According to Gottman, the success of a marriage is dependent in large part on how we live and behave every day, not just on whether we occasionally take time for a midweek date. He suggests couples work consciously to manage their reactions and words, and try to avoid escalating discussions into confrontations, particularly when talking about touchy subjects. He also says that couples should set limits on hurtful behavior from each other. Those that do better are partners who establish high standards for the marriage from the very beginning.

Repairing a Bad Situation

Gottman also says a couple must learn how to repair a bad situation and exit an argument before it gets completely out of control. Repair attempts include things like using humor or reaching out to touch each other to defuse the tension, trying to establish common ground, backing down from a position, or registering appreciation for the other's feelings. He also says happy couples generally focus more on the bright side, and know to go for help early when things get difficult.

Charlie is the master of the repair attempt, often throwing in one of his classic wordplays when conversations get tense. My wise mother told me once that no matter how mad she was at my father, they always felt as if they could still touch each other, sneak a foot over to the other person's side of the bed or lean up against each other—and it was often that little touch that allowed them to make up.

Remarried couples will inevitably struggle—for example, about money issues or harassment from ex-spouses, or resentment and disrespect from children—but most can survive if the couple that holds the entire house of cards together is willing to adapt, stay close, learn tolerance, and develop the skills to resolve their problems. Rigidity, intolerance, withdrawal, and resentment are not helpful. Those who do better are the people who can continue to talk with each other, work out little issues before they become big and overwhelming. I caution myself to watch my impulsive emotionality—those sarcastic comments, eye rolls, exasperated grumbles. In this marriage, I try to be a grown-up in the best sense of the word.

One of the more interesting lessons of remarriage is that the family will usually do better if the individual parents can loosen their grip on their children, something that is often a challenge for people who have survived the tumult of divorce by holding on to their kids for dear life. But in a remarriage, balancing the emotional needs of children and the emotional needs of the adult relationship is key. If one spouse stays deeply enmeshed with his or her children, to the exclusion of his or her mate, the couple is going to have problems. If a husband ignores his children's needs because he is overly attached to his new spouse, he is going to have a different set of problems.

Balancing the Family

Charlie and I were lucky in that we brought almost equal burdens to the marriage. We each have two sons, and the teams of brothers present similar challenges. In families where one parent has brought a very difficult child or a particularly bitter ex-spouse, the other partner can feel unfairly taxed. For us, the family feels balanced, even when we are wrestling with problems.

Somewhere around the middle of our second year, the tension in the house eased. For one thing, the unexpected blessings started coming faster and faster. The boys were helping out in the yard and kitchen with considerably less grumbling. We took a trip to California and the boys worked out a fair and equitable seat-trading system for the rental van entirely on their own, without parental intervention. We had the smoothest trip of our marriage mostly because we were learning to function as a team—all six of us, not just me and Charlie. At the airport two of the boys would help me with the bags in the ticket line, and the other two would head off to get breakfast for the rest of us while Charlie parked the van. Everyone met at the gate in twenty minutes. We don't look like newbies anymore. We are adopting the swagger of veterans.

Today I can sense the growing comfort in the house, the subtle adjustments everyone is making. I am happier as the months go by, feeling more and more like the mom of the hearth in this different but lively and entertaining family. My boys are thriving, my stepsons are thriving, my husband is happy, and the dog doesn't run away anymore. Whether we make it five years, ten years, or—Charlie's goal—fifty years may matter less than how we live each day.

Building the Partnership

I believe that the biggest challenge is to build that marriage partnership—not just for the health of the marriage, but also for the health of the family. And I don't mean just building the love relationship: I mean building a true and equitable partnership in which you work together to make decisions and support each other in managing the family. In which you don't rearrange everyone's schedule at a request from an ex-spouse without consulting your new partner. In which you fight the temptation to isolate yourself when the going gets tough. In which you refuse to allow the household to split into competing camps. In which you stay interested and involved in your stepkids' lives and work to build a bond, even if they do not accept you as an authority. In which you throw bids of affection and connection in everyone's direction every day.

Learning About Herself

In the process of my remarriage, I've learned some eye-opening things about myself: that I will get depressed if I don't fight for the things I need in my life, but that I don't like fights; that my patience is more limited than I ever imagined, now that it has really been put to the test; that I can be judgmental and rigid if I don't watch myself; that I am less resilient than my own children; that living with other people's teenagers is a constant seesaw between love and frustration;

that the woman in the house, no matter how much lip service is paid to alternative lifestyles, will end up making dinner unless someone orders out. That I don't like sharing control but I don't like being responsible for everything, either. That I'm petulant and sometimes seem to nurse my own irritation, as if I need distance but don't know how to ask for it nicely. Sometimes I look in the mirror and wonder if I'm getting less mature every day.

Fortunately, most everybody still seems to like me anyway, which may be the biggest lesson and blessing of this whole enterprise. When I lived alone with my two small boys, I could be the perfect parent—at least in my own estimation. There was no one around to question my judgment on a daily basis. I could indulge my boys, write the rules, nip problems in the bud. Now I'm often challenged on a decision, and sometimes find I don't have a good reason for what I'm planning to do. Sometimes I want to spoil a kid just because I'm too tired to fight. Sometimes I set down a rule and realize, when the kids push back, that it is unnecessary or ridiculous. I've discovered that like most people, I tend toward bossiness and rigidity when I get anxious. I'm getting in touch with the human weaknesses that keep me humble. As a result, I doubt myself more than ever before, but also find I am more thoughtful, more open to other ideas and positions. I'm growing and changing. For someone approaching fifty, whose body and mind wants to calcify rather than stretch, this is challenging indeed.

But most important, I've learned to ride the storm. I've learned to admit my mistakes and then forgive myself and others. I've learned to apologize and to accept apologies and be done with it. I've learned that there will be friction and problems but that they are not, in and of themselves, catastrophes. The catastrophe happens when the family's response is to shut down, get resentful, and stop trying. In time I hope to learn how to detach when I need to take a break, get away, breathe, and regroup.

Making It Fun

When Charlie and I first talked about merging these sets of brothers, among all the plans for housing and schooling and discipline and responsibilities, he kept saying: "Let's make it fun." Sometimes I thought he was crazy. Was doing all that laundry going to be fun? How about the inevitable fights over the remote? The bickering between brothers that would escalate when they didn't feel they could pick on anyone else? But as we started trying to plan for fun, we got better at having a good time together. Big families can be a gas, something our generation seems to have forgotten. Just cramming all of us, our luggage, and the dog into the family van will make somebody start giggling, even if someone else is complaining. So we try to listen to the giggler. Dinner table conversations are often hilarious; there's always something outrageous just bursting to be said, and the bigger the audience, the better the response.

And we don't just plan for fun at holidays and vacations. When we see a tough stretch ahead—exam week, Mom on a deadline, Dad on travel—we schedule in treats or special activities. We consciously build the memories, because that is what we want them to take into adulthood: the lobster night tradition on Cape Cod, the goofy word games we play in the car when we're all bored to tears, the chess tournaments and algebra challenges, the endless rounds of Murder in the Dark.

As Gottman would say and many other researchers have confirmed, you can make your remarriage a self-fulfilling prophecy. If you spend too much time worrying about the weaknesses and failures, you can end up with a failure. Or you can focus on the bright side, the things that are working, and it may turn out to be a success. What I'm learning with this marriage is that it can bump along in all its glorious imperfection, and gradually—if we all keep trying and giving and holding on—it will grow into something strong and resilient.

Something that will provide a foundation for my boys as they grow into men who may try someday to marry and build a family.

Chapter 4

The Children's Point of View

Watching Parents Break Up

Stephanie Staal

When Stephanie Staal was nine years old, a cousin told her the "secret" that her parents were already expecting her before they were married. It was the first time it occurred to her that her parents might not have married for love and that what she had assumed was her happy family might not actually be so happy.

Later, tension between her parents became so strong that her dad created an "office" in the basement where he spent most of his time, including sleeping there. Staal felt it was her responsibility to hold the family together. She found herself acting as mediator between her mom and dad. Then, for a while, her parents seemed to be getting along better and a baby sister was born. Staal hoped having a sister would keep them together, but tension between her parents surfaced again soon after. The tension continued for over a year before the decision to divorce was made. Staal, now an adult, describes what it was like growing up under these circumstances.

When I was five years old, my parents and I moved into a beige split-level home with shuttered windows and a towering maple tree in the front yard. Every fall, the leaves would scatter to the grass, turning into crisp markers of time. Every spring brought the pink bloom of the cherry blossom tree in the backyard, its petals fluttering like snowflakes past the living room window.

My room was painted blue and was right next door to my parents' bedroom. My mother picked out the bed, a starter bed that hovered close to the floor and was shaped like a rectangular box, each side barricaded to prevent accidental falls. My father installed dark blue painted shelves that spanned the

Stephanie Staal, *The Love They Lost: Living with the Legacy of Our Parents' Divorce*. New York: Delacorte Press, 2000.

height of one wall, from ceiling to floor, to organize my stuffed animals, Lego sets, and Beatrix Potter books. I measured my growth in inches every week, standing tall against a measuring tape with a stuffed Snoopy at the top, chest puffed out and stomach sucked in for added height. I slept with a night-light on to chase away the darkness, but sometimes, after a bad dream or when the shadows contorted and flickered, I would wander the ten steps into my parents' bedroom and creep under the covers between them.

Our house was conveniently located within the constellation of the local elementary, junior high, and high schools, and so, this was a neighborhood of families—a neighborhood where fathers mowed the lawn on the weekends, mothers carpooled to soccer games, and during the summer, against a humming backdrop of crickets, children roamed the tree-lined streets until dusk. Life was tidy, calm, and predictable, at least on the outside.

I remember seemingly insignificant events with a weird clarity: My mother bringing a birthday cake decorated with a candy clown to my nursery, school; my father and I spending an afternoon picking out a dress for my mom for Mother's Day; the three of us stopping at a gas station, where I bought a box of pastel-colored Jordan almonds on the way to a weekend in New York City. In broader strokes, I remember that I adored my parents, who were at that point struggling to get a foothold in their respective careers, spending much of their time at work, and I became defined by another popular label coined during my lifetime—the latchkey kid. My childhood seemed filled with pangs of anticipation for when we could all be together, but the thing is, looking back, my parents never really seemed like a unit apart from me—they never held hands or went out to dinner alone. Yes, the house was filled with laughter, camaraderie, and a sense of being complete, but it needed the three of us to work. Us against everyone else.

Somewhere along the way, I started to become aware of a malaise between my parents, a certain chill that came and went. I'm not sure when or why, but gradually the moments of togetherness spread further and further apart until I found myself torn. The configuration of my family had shifted. Instead of being three equal sides of a triangle, we had turned into a straight line, with my parents at either end and me in the middle. On the nights my father worked late, my mother became more animated, as if she had just stumbled in on an unexpected party. We would carry our dinner into the bedroom and lounge on the bed, watching television. On Saturdays, my father and I would go off by ourselves, spending a couple of hours at the library and then eating at a small hole-in-the-wall nearby. At the time, I didn't dwell on this subtle separation. These were my parents, this was my family, and the possibility of divorce only skirted the fringes of my consciousness, a Judy Blume plot twist. I knew something was wrong, but in the absence of any overt hostility, I truly believed everything would be fine. Sort of.

I am nine years old, squeezed in the backseat of my aunt's station wagon with my three cousins. We have been cooped up for a couple of hours and the appeal of a road trip has started to lose its luster. There isn't enough room to pull out a board game, and we are all bored, cranky, and getting on each other's nerves. Too hot—desert-dry heat—and too many bodies. The air conditioner sputters, blows lukewarm air. My cousin leans over and whispers that he knows a secret. I punch him lightly on the arm, demanding he tell. He holds out for as long as he can, which is not very long, and then, with a quick look at the front seat to make sure the adults aren't listening, he gives.

"Your mother was pregnant with you," he smirks, "*before* your parents got married."

Stunned, I need a moment to recover.

"I knew that," I cover up, voice casual. "It's no big deal."

I stare out the window, squinting in the glare as the sun bounces off the glass. With this revelation, the simple fairy tale has turned into a much more complicated maze of emotions. For the very first time—despite the frosty air between my parents—it enters my consciousness that perhaps love has nothing to do with their marriage. Sure enough, I do the math in my head, and my cousin is right. I berate myself for not having figured this out before. "Stupid," I think, "stupid, stupid me."

"You promise you can't tell I told you," my cousin whispers fiercely. "Promise?"

I nod, wishing he would just shut up.

As I try to digest this new information, I feel an unrecognizable flutter in my stomach, which in retrospect I recognize as fear. Such a calculated motivation for marriage, even to my young mind, does not have the diamondlike strength of love. This sudden snag in the fabric of my beliefs makes me realize how easily things can fall apart. Maybe nothing is holding us together. But I had made a promise not to tell, and so I keep this secret to myself, filed away.

By the time I am finishing up elementary school, my parents hardly see each other, and on those occasional nights when the three of us are together, they retreat into silence. My father snaps the newspaper open in front of his face, an insta-wall. My mother immerses herself in a magazine, mechanically eating as her eyes rove across the page. I turn my head back and forth, humming with nervous chatter, until one of them gives me a sharp look. Calm down. Relax. We need quiet. The newspaper goes back up, a page of the magazine turns, and I sit there, with my hands underneath my legs, nearly bursting from confusion and the need to do *something* to fill the air, to get us back to where we were.

The distance that shudders between my parents grows larger and larger, so large it takes a noticeable shape. My father begins to spend more time puttering around the basement. First, he moves his desk into an empty room down there. Then, he starts to decorate, putting up a couple of posters he picked up at the National Gallery of Art as if he is moving into a college dormitory. It doesn't stop there. He buys a dresser, followed by his own refrigerator, and finally a bed. Soon, after dinner he is disappearing behind the closed door of his "study"; the acrid scent of cigar smoke sneaks out from beneath the door, but my father does not emerge until the next morning. The house is now divided, and I travel between my two parents—upstairs, downstairs, upstairs—like a desperate emissary of goodwill.

Then, suddenly, or so it seems, everything is fine. When I am eleven years old, I return from spending the summer with my grandparents, and my parents arrive at the airport to pick me up. At the baggage carousel, as my father heaves my suitcase off the conveyor belt, my mother leans toward me and with a wide grin announces she is pregnant. The comforting thought that, finally, I have an ally overpowers any primal wave of sibling rivalry. The three of us are once again linked, by the excitement over my mother's pregnancy. In the following months, as her belly begins to swell and grow, I step in with a frightening officiousness. I demand the exclusive right to choose the baby's name, and after poring over books, come up with such exotic appellations as "Flora" and "Dominique." I flip through pregnancy manuals, brow furrowed in concentration, learning all I can about such things as amniocentesis, epidurals, and spina bifida. I worry about chromosomal deficiencies and limb growth. I choose the wallpaper for the baby's room, and on a weekend afternoon, I help my father paste it up. And when my sister Caroline is born, a little blue but perfectly healthy, I feel such relief that now, thank God, I am not alone with the burden of keeping this family together. The moment I see her, small and wrinkled with a thick cap of dark hair, I fall in love. With the four of us, it looks like the clamp will hold.

Nowadays, images of my early childhood come through like bad videotape—the sound and picture, fuzzy with static, keep dropping out, leaving me unable to get inside that little girl's head. What does seem clear is that the quality of my memory was forever changed in the span of one night when I was twelve years old. I often wish the situation were reversed, that I could remember clearly what life was like before the divorce, and lose what happened after in a vague haze. But unfortunately, that's not the case. Memories from my parents' breakup spring from dark corners of my mind with a brilliant clarity, every detail permanently etched with a sharpness that still brings tears to my eyes, even today.

It's late autumn, and the leaves have transformed into cool fire, all burnt reds and oranges. My mother has gone out of the country on a business trip, something she has started to do more often of late. My father tells me he has to do some research at the library, and shortly after dinner, he puts on the blue leather jacket my mother gave him for Christmas and walks out the door. It is a typical school night, I suppose: I chat on the phone with a friend about teachers, boys, the scary wonders of starting junior high. I am almost bubbling with good mood, and before I put my sister to bed, I dance across the living room with her bunched up in my arms while the radio belts out some Top Forty tune, Madonna's "Lucky Star," I think. Afterward, I go downstairs and splay out on my stomach in front of the television to do homework. The front door opens, and I see my father's shoes peeking through the staircase railing. He walks down the stairs, with such slow, heavy steps that I twist around and sit up, and as soon as I see him, I know something is wrong. His face is flat, ashen.

He looks at me, spurts out, "Your mother," then chokes back the rest.

I turn to ice, skin tingly. "She's dead," I think. The room is spinning and I feel this overwhelming desire to stop time right then and there, to not know what I'm about to know. Nevertheless, a voice, my voice, asks, "What is it?"

He crosses the room and crumples into a tan easy chair. "She's been having an affair," he says, and as if the act of uttering the words has stolen his last bit of strength, he collapses with his head in his hands, sobbing.

Back then, I had never seen my father cry before. He was always the rational one, the responsible one, solid and stoic, and the sight of him, of the red bruises forming around his eyes from his tears, paralyzes me. I can't move. I can't speak. Finally, I pull myself up off the floor and walk over to him, then pat his shoulder awkwardly as he spits out, "You love someone and this is what they do to you," over and over again, a hoarse, bitter mantra that makes me want to run away.

The television is still on, canned laughter hanging in the air. I sit on the arm of the chair. With his every jagged heave, I pat, and after what seems like forever, my father gets up and goes to his room in the basement. I go to my bedroom and crawl under the covers, but I'm too dizzy and numb to sleep. I have no one to talk to. I stare at the ceiling wide-eyed and then get up and quietly walk into my mom's bedroom to use the phone. With the number pad lighting up the darkness, I sit on the edge of the bed and call my grandparents. When I hear their voices, sounding so close even though they are thousands of miles away, the cold knot I've been feeling begins to loosen and unravel. Only then do I start to cry, barely getting out what I believe my father has told me.

"I think my parents are getting a divorce."

My parents didn't get a divorce, at least not right away. A couple of days later, my father, sister, and I go to pick up my mother at the airport. Her face, pale and drawn, emerges from the crowd surging off the plane. She doesn't look at my father, but comes forward to give my sister and me a hug. I stay rigid in her embrace, but something cracks inside, because this is my mother, not some cardboard villain intent on destroying the family. She tucks a strand of hair behind my ear, and looks away. We drive home. I sit in the front seat. My father turns on the radio. Everyone is quiet, and I stare out the window. Highway. Trees. Night. Back at the house, we sit in the living room, backs straight and hands folded, each of us inhabiting our own private section of the couch, until my parents finally tell me things are up in the air. "We just don't know what is going to happen," says my mother. "Your father and I have to figure this out." The tension wraps around the room. "Well, nothing is going to be decided tonight," says my father, jaw set. "We might as well go to bed." We all go to our separate rooms and shut our doors.

Actually, nothing is decided for a year—probably the most excruciating year of my life. The possibility of divorce hangs over each day, and I wake up in the morning not knowing what to expect. I wander nervously through the house, constantly monitoring the conflict meter: My mother moves out, moves back in. My father wants a divorce, then wants to try and work things out. I mediate, the twelve-year-old marriage counselor, and when my mother is swinging toward leaving, I take her aside and plead with her to "focus on what's important." When my father's mood darkens, I insist, "She feels like you don't love her." I am passing along impressions, advice, messages, encouraging them to go out to dinner, maybe spend some time alone to rekindle the romance. But this is a different kind of combustible environment, one of resentment unbound, and sometimes they clash with such fury that I want to duck for cover.

Yet just as bad as the eruptions of fighting between my parents—those fiery rounds of accusations fueled by the slightest comment—are the periods of forced family cheer, those times when we sit and smile around the dinner table, engaging in stilted conversation, all the while gritting our teeth from the strain of trying too hard. I start to spend less time at home, to stay away from my parents as much as possible. We are all wilting under the pressure. I remember one evening, after I've attempted to wheedle my mother to let me go see a movie with a friend rather than eat dinner at home, she pulls me close and hisses, "Don't you want this to work?" And I do, so I stay without complaint. I desperately want to keep my family whole, want my parents to stay together. But not like this. Not like this.

One night, I creep out of my bedroom, awakened by my parents' fighting. Suddenly my father rushes down the hallway carrying armfuls of my mother's clothing. He kicks open the front door and tosses her dresses into the front yard. They sail into the darkness for a moment, then drift down like colorful parachutes to fall limp on the grass. My mother follows him out the door and stands with her arms crossed under the yellow streetlamp, watching as he brings out more clothes, time and again, until there are no clothes left inside the house. Outside, amidst a lawn sprayed with clothing, their renewed screaming rises up in the darkness. From the kitchen window, I see my mother open the door of her Volvo and start the engine, drowning out my father's curses. She sits in her car, thinking, waiting, before finally pulling out of the driveway. My stomach drops, as if her departure has pushed me over and I am tumbling fast down an endless tunnel. I want them both to stop, to go away. My bare feet move silently across the tile and, holding my breath, I lock the front door. I sit in the hallway, my knees tight against my chest, shaking. My father pounds on the door with his fist a minute later. He jiggles the knob, threatens and cajoles, then finally retrieves the spare key from the backyard. When he comes in, anger and frustration etched on his face, he says to me, "Don't you ever do that again," and walks away. A couple of days later, my mother moves back in, and we start all over again.

Winter. Spring. Summer. I turn thirteen, and as soon as school is out, I escape to my grandparents' house across the country for three months. Almost the day I step off the plane, I become a different person. My chronic stomachaches subside. I feel light and, for the first time in almost a year, happy. My grandparents and I have always been close, but this particular summer, they are my saviors. We spend lazy days on the beach, watching the sunset, camping, and, best of all, having long conversations—real discussions, not the exchanges encased in a hard shell of defensiveness I have grown used to. I even successfully block out the life waiting for me back at home, until a couple of weeks before I am about to leave, my grandfather asks me to take a walk with him on the beach. We crawl over the rocky sand, then rest on a gnarled piece of driftwood as the sun lowers in the sky. I can sense that this walk has a purpose.

And I'm right. I've become skillful at recognizing the facial expressions, the tone of voice, all the telltale signs that mark the preface of painful words. I steel myself. My grandfather looks at me, and speaks. *Your parents have finally decided to get a divorce. Your mother is moving out.* I listen, feeling nothing, absolutely nothing, least of all surprised. "I wasn't supposed to tell you, they didn't want me to," he says, squeezing my hand. "But I didn't think that was right. I thought you should know." I latch on to this last bit—not tell me?—astonished that my parents can treat this as a private matter that doesn't include anyone else. For the remainder of my visit, anger and dread intertwine. When my grandparents drop me off at the airport, I clutch on to them until the final boarding call, not wanting to get on that plane. I cry for the entire six-hour flight, sobbing so hard that my eyes swell to slits, so hard that the woman in the seat next to me leans over and tries to comfort me. She thinks someone has died.

When I get home, my mother informs me she is leaving in a week and taking my sister with her, that it's easier that way. My father stands by the window holding Caroline, who sleeps peacefully against his shoulder, their faces iced by the early morning sunlight. I can't even contemplate the absence of not only my mother but my sister. The days of family are now numbered. The word "divorce" is never mentioned, but implicit is the understanding that this time, she is not coming back. I accept the news with a simple nod of the head. No protests, no angry words, no attempts at convincing them to change their minds. It is as if some tap has been tightened shut.

There is nothing worse, I think, than when your parents break your heart.

Having to Move

Melanie, Annie, and Steven Ford as told to Jan Blackstone-Ford

Melanie, Annie, and Steven Ford are now step-siblings. They have written a book called My Parents Are Divorced, Too: A Book for Kids by Kids, *to tell other kids what it was like for them when their parents divorced. In this excerpt, they talk about some of the concerns they had when they realized that divorce also meant they would have to move. Topics they discuss include leaving their friends, living in two houses, and adjusting to their new situation.*

Having to Move

Why Do I Have to Move? Melanie: I didn't understand why I had to leave my house and my room. Even though we moved only a mile away, I still had to leave my room and my dad. My parents were the ones getting the divorce, not me. Why did I have to leave? I didn't understand that when your parents get a divorce, so do you. I didn't understand why my dad wasn't coming with us. I knew they were getting a divorce. I didn't get what "divorce" meant. I hated the whole thing.

Annie: My mom and I moved two hours away from our old home. It was a lot different from where I used to live. I liked it much better. See, we moved away from my stepfather. I didn't like him that much, so I wasn't sad to go. I felt like I could start all over. I missed my old friends, but I made new friends real fast.

Steven: I was so young I don't remember moving out.

Annie: Moving doesn't have to be that bad. At first, I didn't want to move. My mom asked me to give it a chance, and

Melanie, Annie, and Steven Ford as told to Jan Blackstone-Ford, *My Parents Are Divorced, Too: A Book for Kids by Kids*. Washington, DC: Magination Press, 1997.

then see how I felt. I did give it a chance, and I liked it much better. That's what I would tell my friend to do. If you really don't like it, then you have to tell your mom or dad, and maybe they can change something. I mean, they probably won't live together again, but maybe they could help you like the place better. Maybe they can take you out to see what there is to do in the new town.

Melanie: When my friend Jill moved here after her parents got a divorce, she liked her old home better. She talked about it all the time. Now she is used to it here, but it has been two years.

Will I Lose My Old Friends? Annie: I made my old friends into pen pals. I love to get mail! We write back and forth all the time. It's fun because I never used to get letters, and now I do. My old friends come to visit me in the summer. It has been a long time, and we still write, and they always come to stay with me for a few days. Sometimes even their mom comes. We all have a great time.

Changing Houses

Where Do I Live, and When? Melanie: We live in a very small town. When my parents first separated, my mom, Steven, and I moved just a mile away from my dad. In the beginning, we switched back and forth every other day. That was hard because I kept having to pack up every day to go to the other place, and it was very confusing. When I was in the third grade, I sometimes left my homework at the other house. I fell behind in school. Then when my dad got married again, we decided to switch houses every other week. I like that better because I still see both my parents, but now I know where I will be. We switch on Fridays. I have a room at both houses. All the parents get along, so if I want to see the other parent, I just ask and go. The biggest problem used to be that I missed my mom when I was at my dad's, and I missed my dad when I was at my mom's.

Steven: I have a friend, Sam, whose parents got a divorce. He had to live with his father, who lived two hours away, and his brother had to live with his mother. That was very bad. He missed his brother and his mom. Sometimes he was glad his brother lived somewhere else because then he couldn't beat him up! But he still missed him. Now his father has moved back to our town, so Sam lives with his mom and his brother, and they can see their father anytime they want. It was just too hard the other way. He likes it better now.

Annie: Lots of my friends' parents are divorced. Some live with just their mom. One lives with just his dad. I have a friend who lives with his grandparents. I have two other friends who live with both their mom and their dad, like Melanie and Steven do—one week at mom's, and the other week at dad's. I live with my mom and Larry most of the time. I see my dad every other weekend.

I Wish I Were Somewhere Else! Melanie: I'm not sure you are ever happy all the way with where you live after a divorce. Things happen and you wish you were at the other house. Like when we go to my mom's for the weekend, and my dad goes to a baseball game, or something else I'd like to do. But I have to stay at my mom's because we haven't seen each other in a week. But sometimes we go to special places with my mom, too, so I guess it all evens itself out. It takes a while, but you get used to it.

Bringing Parents Together in a "Happy" Divorce

Ilana Kramer

When Ilana Kramer was three years old, her mother packed her two daughters into a broken-down station wagon and headed across the country to New Jersey while her father remained in California. Partly due to the geographical distance between them, Kramer's parents managed to maintain a sense of "family" for the girls, a unique feat to accomplish after a divorce.

Now in her twenties, Kramer recalls many happy memories of family time during the years she was growing up. The family frequently vacationed together, her parents enjoying one another's company as well as the children. When step-parents came into the picture, they also became part of the happy family, sharing trips, holidays, and long distance phone conversations. When Kramer consulted her parents for their point of view, they told her that her childhood wasn't as rosy as she remembers it. But hearing their version couldn't cloud the happy memories she had retained.

I am a wildfire of curls and freckles, sitting in the backseat of my mother's broken-down station wagon. We are parked by the side of the road heading east, somewhere between California and New Jersey, and all I know is that I am three years old and on a terrific adventure. I watch as one of our tires bounds down a ravine, a skittish jackrabbit. Heat and fumes are rising from our hood, making the skyline tremble ahead. My sister, two years my senior and already in charge, is sitting in the front seat.

My mother is outside the car, frantic; she is looking for a spare she knows she doesn't have, but she is looking just the

Ilana Kramer, "Bringing Parents Together in a 'Happy' Divorce," *Lilith*, vol. 29, spring 2004, p. 20.

same. She and my father have just divorced, and now she has two daughters to raise and a car to push to the other side of the country.

Five years later, the chaos has subsided in a rare and curious way. I am on a family vacation at Universal Studios with my mom, my sister, and my dad. My sister and I are biting the bottoms of sugar cones and sucking out the soft ice cream. We are all waiting on line for an Alfred Hitchcock ride, when the attendant asks for a male participant. My mom immediately volunteers my father. Twenty minutes later my father stands on stage wide-eyed in a dress, playing the mother's role in "Psycho." When he's asked to introduce his family, we proudly stand up from the audience and wave. To onlookers in the park, we might look like your typical nuclear family, but if someone asked me for the low-down, I would have to explain I come from a happy divorce.

Divorced, but Still a Family

Growing up, my divorced family was unusual. My parents made a decision to make our family still act as a "family." While my friends in "intact" families hung out with both parents, and my friends of divorce had strict separate time with each parent, we fell into an uncharted no-man's land. Since my two parents lived with an entire country dividing them, this resulted in a lot of family vacations. My mother and father planned lobster dinners in Connecticut, swimming with dolphins in Key West, skiing in the Catskills, and endless Amtrak trips to Florida to my paternal grandparents. With my mom, sister, and me all in a king-sized bed in one hotel room and my dad snoring next door in another, I felt my family all around me. Despite my having no recollection of their marriage together, I have a lot of memories of my parents, well, together. And our arrangement didn't end when my mother remarried.

Once we became a blended family, my dad would not only call on the phone for my sister, mom, and me, but would often ask to speak to his "husband-in-law," my step-dad. They would chat about business, cars, and exchange jokes. One Thanksgiving on the East Coast, my father and step-dad took my sister, step-siblings, and me to the Macy's parade in New York City. When my dad got remarried, during my first year of college, his new wife became yet another addition to the family. I remember my dad and step-mom staying at our home in New Jersey (with my mom and step-dad); in the mornings, we would all swarm around the table like fruit flies for lox-and-bagel breakfasts.

My college graduation this past spring was the real clincher. There was an option for parents to stay in the college dormitories, so my mother secured two rooms next door to each other. While friends maneuvered social plans to minimize their divorced parents' interactions, my four parents were coordinating theirs. My mom and step-mom were fussing over hors d'oevres parties between the two rooms, while my step-dad helped my father reconfigure the single dorm beds in his room to make up a larger one. Sunday morning, when I checked in with all of my parents in the dorm, I saw my step-dad watching a baseball game and my dad writing out bills at a study table, tufts of white hair flying out behind each ear and in one of his striped long t-shirts that my mother called his "nightgowns." My mom and step-mother were kibbitzing [chatting] making fun of my father together.

Walking out of the elevator, my family memories hit me like flashcards turning over: the time we drove in my grandparents' car in Florida, my grandpa stubborn, lost, and nearly deaf in the front seat, my mom and dad laughing hysterically in the back; or the time my mom threw pillows at my dad, hollering to him, "I hate men!" after an especially bad date. I think of my family holding hands, walking in to the song "We are Family!" at the reception after my bat mitzvah.

And then I think back to my father taking me to my JCC nursery school classroom to say goodbye to my friends before my postdivorce journey east. I remember my father was a giant then, and I reached my hand up to hold his thick fingers and watch his peppery moustache, and I felt small and uncertain. Are all these memories, then, what comprise my definition of a happy divorce?

I know I'm simplifying a complex process. Every moment didn't sparkle with Brady-Bunch zing. I missed my father at soccer games and summer school plays. On vacations, when both parents tucked me into bed, I felt a pinch of that childhood gingerbread dream that maybe, just maybe my parents would fall back in love. And I imagine that in my own absorbed and eager youth, it was difficult in quiet ways for them both, especially my mother, the sensitive one who singlehandedly raised my sister and me. But I believe my parents sustained our family unit in a unique and inventive way.

Her Parents' Point of View

When I ask my father about it, he remembers how difficult it was when the divorce first happened. Apparently it never occurred to him that by separating from my mother he might live 3,000 miles away from his children. He feared we wouldn't remain close. That didn't happen. When I questioned my parents recently, he had great memories of fun times with my sister and me. On winter break from college, the three of us driving down the Baja peninsula in Mexico to drink pina coladas and set off fireworks ("Girls, don't tell your mother"). The time he helped me catch a six-foot sailfish. Or how my dad would give us the same lecture at the beginning of every summer to Be Nice to his long-term girlfriend ("She loves you very much, girls"). Meanwhile, we plotted like devilish twins, buying whoopee cushions and black soap, all for a woman who, in truth, did appear to love us even though we seemed to need to play tricks on her to keep solidarity with our mother. In a way, while my mother dealt with the less-glamorous tasks of raising us during the school year, my father was able to reap the benefits of having smart, well-adjusted little daughters fly out to him every summer.

Perhaps it was because my parents had a great expanse of geography between them that helped to cool the landscape of hostility inherent in divorce. Maybe it was that they divorced when I was an infant, and neither remarried until I was a teen, enabling them to free up time for vacations. Or maybe, by living with distance between them my sister and I could easily adopt the lifestyle and values of my mother, which may have conflicted with my father's and caused confusion if we were all located in the same town. Whatever the case, my parents shared a love for large mishpocha gatherings and—most importantly—for their children. When my mom calls me now in Manhattan for Saturday morning "Plan Ahead" lectures or my dad calls late at night to mimic impressions of my mother fretting, "Your father . . . ," both calls make me sigh and laugh.

I shared my perspective of my parents' divorce with my mother the other evening in a phone call. Turns out that her reality was less sugar-coated than I'd perceived it. In interest of full disclosure, I share with you the e-mail I got the next morning from my Mom:

> Lani. . . Was thinking about our conversation . . . I guess it changed your idea of a "happy" divorce a little and I'm sorry, but the truth is that no divorce is painless or easy. I'm glad your perception of it was happy. That shows that despite my stress, you still perceived things between Dad and me as not too bad. Guess that was good for your development.
>
> Divorced people go through the same stages as grief/loss people do: shock, denial, anger, sadness, and finally resolution. It can take many years to get through, particularly if one person is at a financial disadvantage. Also it's a loss of dreams and hopes. When you marry you think it is forever,

and then it's not. The way I answered you last night was purely honest, and maybe you are now old enough to hear the truth. When I was a single-parent, I was in survival mode, both financially and emotionally. I sometimes acted in ways that were not always sincere, but I did it to survive. When I met your stepfather, some of the survival mode left, and then it didn't matter. Does this all make sense to a 22-year-old? Don't know. Well, you asked.

Again, let me know your plans for Friday. I have a 3 p.m. nail appt. but will be done by 4.

Love, Mom

Getting to Know Mom Again

Valerie Kaufmann

When Valerie Kaufmann was five years old, her parents separated. By the time she was six, her father had full custody. Her mother disappeared out of their lives, and Kaufmann didn't see her again for six years. In this article, written at age eleven, Kaufmann talks about what it was like not to see her mother for so long and then have her suddenly reappear.

The court ordered that Kaufmann and her siblings have regular visits with their mother. The children complied, but the visits were not how Kaufmann had imagined them. She had hoped for a joyful reunion, fulfilling her fantasy of what she thought a mother should be like. However, there were no happy hugs and catching up with the lives of the children who had been so abruptly deserted. Her mother never offered an explanation for why she had left, or apologized for having been gone so long, and didn't seem interested in what they were like or what they had been doing. Kaufmann saw her mother as a giant disappointment. The court-ordered visits continued for a while, until Kaufmann refused to go. Her mother stopped seeing all of the children then, and she may or may not see them again. Kaufmann lives happily with her father and stepmother and doesn't want to see her biological mother any more.

When I was 5, my parents separated, and my brother Eddie, 2, sister Victoria, 7, and I were shuffled around between relatives because our parents lived in different houses. For a while, we lived with our mother, and I vaguely remember living with our grandmother. When I was 6, our father got full custody.

For a while, my mother visited, but her visits became less frequent before stopping altogether. I can't remember the mo-

Valerie Kaufman, "Giving Up on Mom," *Girl's Life*, June 2002, pp. 88–89.

ment I knew she was gone for good. But I know my dad explained she had left and he wasn't sure if she'd be back. I was upset but too young to really understand the scope of it all.

Eventually, though, I got mad. I thought about what it'd be like to have a mother and wondered how she could leave her kids. I waited for her to contact me. But I never heard from her—not on holidays, birthdays or ever. I could barely remember what she looked like. I knew she had long, black hair, but that's about it. It's not that I missed her, really. I missed the idea of having a mother to tuck me in at night and talk to me about my period and how to deal with boys.

Last year, my parents' divorce was finalized, and my dad remarried a woman named Valerie, like me! She became a mom to me, driving me to school, helping with homework, watching dance recitals. We talked about the things I imagined mothers talk to their daughters about. Like, Valerie told me never to obsess over boys or chase them. She's talked to me about puberty and other girly stuff.

After Six Years, Her Mother Wants to See Her

And then, this year, out of the blue, my father told Eddie, Victoria and me that our mother wanted to see us. My reaction? Anger. She'd left for six years with no explanation. Why should I care about her when my feelings, obviously, meant nothing to her? I had a new mother, so why should I care about seeing this person I didn't even know?

But the court system insisted we meet with her, and a judge would decide whether we'd keep visiting. Sure, part of me thought it might work—we could get to know each other again. Maybe I could get an answer to the question that plagued me: Why did she leave?

My sibs were happy and seemed willing to give our mother a chance. I, on the other hand, had many doubts. I didn't feel like she had the right to waltz back into our lives. I told my dad this, and he said I had to see her at least once. He promised that if it went badly, he'd step in. Even with his promise, I was so nervous the night before we saw her that I was sick to my stomach. What would we say to each other?

The courts appointed a supervisor to be there when we met our mother, and it was at this supervisor's office that we met the next day. When I walked in, my mother was already there. She had the same long, black hair but had definitely gained weight. She looked up and cried. I just stood there, feeling weird.

Not Like A Fantasy

It was not like my fantasy—no hugs and no joyful reunion. I couldn't hold back and asked right away, "Why did you leave us?" She was quiet, and then she explained that she woke up every morning thinking about getting visitation rights but "just didn't." I was so disappointed. That was no explanation.

The visit was an hour, and it's pretty much a blur. But she told me she missed us, and she said she was going to buy things for us. She didn't ask questions about what we'd been doing all these years. It was like listening to a stranger. There was no connection for me at all. Besides, Valerie was my mom. That night in bed, I decided my mother could never make things better and I didn't want to spend any more time with her.

Only, my mother got visitation rights. I was forced to see her a few hours every two weeks. My father told the courts I didn't want to go, but they didn't listen. I had to spend time with her, and there was nothing we could do.

On the next visit, I brought photos. I wanted her to see the things she had missed. In part, I thought she should know about us, but it was also to make her feel guilty. She looked at the pictures but didn't say much. Instead, she talked about her life. My mother had a new husband and 2-year-old daughter, which made me angrier. Why was she taking care of a new daughter but not us? Even worse, she had lived just 15 minutes from us the whole time!

When she took us to her house, I'd go straight to the computer while she hung with my sibs. They'd play board games and cook together, and I'd just sit there. My sister Victoria got mad and told me I should try to get to know my mother.

I might have given her more of a chance if she'd explained why she left. I also wanted an apology. Some part of me wanted her to ask me why I was ignoring her and try to make things better. But, again, she did nothing. With every visit, I was more convinced she didn't care and wasn't worth the effort.

Not Seeing Her Mom Anymore

After a month, her visitation rights increased to weekly. I wanted to spend no time with this woman and, suddenly, I was forced to see her even more. Then, the court system gave her the right to call nightly. So she'd call, and I'd refuse to talk. After a week of avoiding her calls, she picked us up for a visit and, as soon as we got in the car, she screamed out that I was hurting her feelings. Did she forget about the six years she was gone? She missed my entire childhood! Eventually, she realized I wasn't going to change my mind. So she wrote a letter to the judge, saying I didn't have to see her anymore. It was a huge relief.

But, after that, she stopped seeing Eddie and Victoria, too. Week after week, she made excuses for why she couldn't see them. I felt bad because my siblings were hurt all over again. But they soon came to see our mother is just selfish and not worth the time. Sometimes, I think the only reason she wanted to see us was to make my dad angry and that it had nothing to do with us.

About seven months after our first visit, the court system officially took all visitation rights away from my mother. At this point, none of us wanted to see her. Also, she'd missed a couple court dates, which only supported the judge's decision to take away her visitation rights altogether. She can't legally spend time with us unless my father gives her permission. So far, she hasn't asked, and I doubt she ever will.

It's been a few months since I last saw my mother. I'm still happily living with my dad and stepmother, and I definitely consider Valerie to be my mom. She's there whenever I need to talk to her, and she was great through the whole ordeal with my biological mother. She stayed out of it when she could, but she listened to me when I wanted to talk about it.

As for my mother, I do worry about running into her since she lives so close by. If I were to see her at the mall or something, I'd run the other way. The bottom line is, she is a giant disappointment to me. I'm glad I confronted her and told her I didn't want to see her anymore. It's sad that I'll never trust my mother, but it's a relief to know who she really is—a selfish person. I don't hold onto thoughts of who she ought to be and what I might be missing out on. I also take comfort knowing that if I had to do it all over again, I wouldn't do my part any differently.

If you are in a similar situation, it's really important to talk with people you trust and who are willing to listen to your thoughts and feelings. Most important, I hope you understand that none of it is your fault. I used to wonder if my mother left because of something I had said or done, but my dad helped me understand it had nothing to do with me. I was so young, and the problems in the house were between them. I've talked with my aunt and stepmother, who both encouraged me to feel my anger but then move on. So that's what I'm doing now—I'm moving on. And, believe me, you can too.

Meeting Her Father for the First Time at Age Twenty-Seven

Ava Chin

Ava Chin's mother and father had been in a relationship for a while when her mother became pregnant. It was the late 1960s, a time when abortion was illegal and unmarried mothers were frowned upon. Chin's father already had two daughters from a previous marriage and wasn't interested in more children. He agreed to marry her mother and then quickly divorce her in order to legitimatize the baby, but he did not intend to be part of the family.

By the time Chin entered the world, her father was gone from her mother's life. Chin grew up absorbing a feeling of anger toward her father from her mother's family. At the age of twenty-seven, Chin finally had a meeting with her two half sisters. They encouraged her to arrange a meeting with their father, and she finally did so. In this essay, Chin talks about her fatherless childhood and about what it was like to finally meet her father so many years later.

My father left us when my mother was pregnant with me, and for many years I searched for clues of him. These were the only tangible objects he left behind: a faded black-and-white photograph of him circa 1969, smiling widely, seated in a rocking chair at my grandparents' house—an image later burned by my mother with a kitchen match when he refused to pay child support; a stuffed koala bear, presented to my mother in the early days of their courtship, with black plastic paws and a silver chain around its neck, which I slept

Ava Chin, *Split: Stories from a Generation Raised on Divorce*. New York: Contemporary Books, 2002.

with and drooled on as a child until the fake fur matted into hard lumps under my mouth; the sexy, diamond-cut engagement ring I had never before seen on my mother's slim finger, shined the day she sold it for less than its true value in order to pay the rent; a simple gold cross presented to me by my father's mother when I was an infant, devoid of decoration, hung on a tiny gold chain, and stored away in a plain white box. Though I have had it for many years, I have still never worn it.

Fantasies About an Absent Father

I tried many times to visualize what my father looked like, but there was no tangible image to grab hold of, besides the burned photograph, which didn't exist anymore except in my memory. All that remained were leftover feelings of hatred, anger, and betrayal from my mother's family; a cold silence whenever his name was mentioned; a few disapproving looks; and the perceptible feeling that some secretly felt sorry for me despite my good grades, creativity, and thin-girl prettiness. It was a wound I carried with me through my teenage years, and into my twenties, dating boys who couldn't stop my pain and who eventually left defeated by my past. It was the wound that made me a writer, according to one professor in college, and I wielded it like a trophy that doubled as a weapon whenever anyone got too close.

Like many abandoned children, I created an elaborate fantasy about how I might one day meet my father, which changed and shifted through the years like my own developing body. In the earliest version, from a childhood informed by too much film and television, he would be laid prostrate on his deathbed and call for me, much like Pharaoh did for Moses in *The Ten Commandments*. He'd repeat my name insistently until his final breath.

In another version, I'd arrive unannounced to a family function at one of those Hong Kong–style banquet halls in

Chinatown; I would be well dressed and half a foot taller than I actually grew to be. I'd dramatically throw aside the veil that covered my face, and surprise everyone by revealing myself as his daughter. No one would be able to dispute it, one look at me would be confirmation enough. (I was reminded constantly by my mother's family that I looked "exactly like him.")

In yet another version—imagined in my early post-collegiate days when I volunteered as a labor organizer in Chinatown—I would be abducted by gang members controlled by my father's well-connected family and we'd meet face-to-face, father and daughter. He'd be shocked, angry at his thugs, and embarrassed before setting me free. We'd cry, embrace, and catch up on lost years. (This I call the "Mob Princess" version.)

Though the details varied from year to year, from version to version, the central story line was always the same: repentant and ashamed, he would beg forgiveness and recognize me as the long-lost valued daughter he'd so actively overlooked. But the real events as they played out that led to my finding him were actually quieter, humbler, and more dramatic than I could ever have anticipated.

Conceived Out of Wedlock

The details behind my parents' meeting are infamous in our family history. The setting was New York's Chinatown in the late 1960s. My father, the first son in an important Chinese-American family, was the number-two lawyer in the community. He had political aspirations and, at the time when he met my mother, was seeking to run for the state assembly as a Democrat. He was separated from his first wife, a biracial beauty from Beijing, and had two daughters from this marriage. My mother, who was vivacious and also very beautiful, had just been crowned Miss Chinatown. She had a master's degree and was an elementary school teacher. Their sudden relationship was passionate and disastrous, like most relationships between politicians and beauty queens. He was older—thirty-six to her twenty-three—and closer to my grandparents' age than to hers. My mother was enthralled with him, indeed the legends of my father's charm are undeniable, even by those most disapproving of his actions. He owned a popular after-hours club on Bleecker Street in the West Village that some still remember to this day, and if you ask him about it, he can rattle off stories about Jimi Hendrix and Janis Joplin who used to frequent the bar as their post-gig hangout. Though my mother doesn't like to talk about their relationship, according to my grandmother, he did the proverbial sweeping her off her feet, and they were soon engaged to be married.

The rest of the story is rather blurry, but this is what I have gathered, and given what I now know about relations between men and women, seems to make the most sense. While engaged, they became pregnant with me. My mother, who wanted a child, was overjoyed. My father, who already had children, was not. According to my grandmother, he pressured her to get an abortion. This being 1969, and abortion illegal, she refused. Sometime after realizing that he couldn't change her mind, he shut off as men sometimes do—seemingly without feeling or outward signs of remorse. He said he no longer loved her. I believe that he fell in love with another woman. Falling in love with other women while he was already involved in a committed relationship would be a running motif in my father's life, but my mother wasn't yet privy to that information.

Pregnant and ashamed, my mother ran away from her family, and for several days her two older brothers searched for her, through Flushing, Kew Gardens, and Jamaica, Queens. My grandmother, who herself came from an influential Chinese banking family, and was born in this country and raised with money and the church in her bones, demanded a meeting with my father. He agreed to meet her with his lawyer.

There must have been several hours of negotiating, which I can only imagine: my father, lean, in his ubiquitous suit, arguing that the disgrace would taint his career, his lawyer listening, giving occasional legal advice; my small grandmother, usually so accommodating, resolute and firm as she defended not only her daughter, but her family's reputation as well. She would later profess to a hatred of all lawyers that I had assumed was omnipresent, but that I now realize must have been the result of this meeting.

Finally, they came to an agreement: there would be a brief marriage, followed by a quick divorce. According to my grandmother, my father dramatically swore he would never lay eyes on the child as long as he lived. In that respect, unlike the broken engagement and the promise of love everlasting he promised to my mother and the two other wives after her, he was almost true to his word. Aside from the time in which my mother visited him with me, an infant in her arms, the next time I was to meet him would be when I was twenty-seven years old.

Meeting Her Sisters for the First Time

In the summer of 1997, I met my sisters for the first time. They were the daughters from my father's first marriage. Meeting them was the realization of a long-held fantasy—growing up an only child, I had always wanted sisters. The one closest in age to me, Kristine, was small, lively, and personable. She worked in magazine publishing like I did (she was a photo editor at *Condè Nast Traveler*), and I felt an instant kinship with her. Then there was Nadine, who was pleasant but distant; she'd known all of the stepmothers (three) and numerous girlfriends, and already had another half-sister and a host of ex-stepsisters. She had the wary air of the disinterested that either meant she was very interested or else really couldn't care less. When you've been exposed to a parent's numerous failed relationships ever since you were ten, I suppose you learn not to get too close.

At our first meeting together we had dinner at a French bistro on Twenty-Third Street. I felt light-headed, almost giddy. Being with my two older sisters gave a sense of sibling connectedness that I had never felt before; it meant more to me than I think they realized. I liked the familiarity they had with each other, the friendly banter, the mutual support. They said that they had told "Dad" about me and that he was very excited to meet. They wanted to know when I was going to call him. I was polite, but gently pushed the questions aside. Thankfully, they let me change the subject.

I was surprisingly resistant to the idea of meeting him. Now that I was so close, something very stubborn within me was refusing to do it, and I wasn't exactly sure why. Before, I had always had the fear that he'd reject me. (The idea of this type of double rejection is something that even now makes me shudder to think about.) But the fact that he had expressed a desire to meet took that fear away, and instead, I was left with anger. Where had he been all that time, and why hadn't *he* come to meet *me?* Why did I have to be the one who took the risk and approach him? Wasn't he the adult? Shouldn't he be the one to get in touch? I debated back and forth like this for several months.

I felt, in a way, that my very identity was being threatened. I was, after all, the girl who had never met her father. I was someone everyone felt sorry for, but admired for being strong. It allowed me to feel righteous about the harshness of the world, to feel that I was somehow better for dealing so well with the burden. I had grown very used to this chip I'd had on my shoulder for so long. I wasn't quite ready to give it up.

A Blank Page Where A Father Should Be

When I was a child, my close friends would ask if I hated my father.

I used to think it was an odd question. *Hate* was too strong an emotion for a man I had never met. Whenever I thought of him, I drew a complete blank. Like a big white space in the middle of a sentence signifying a missing word—a word like "love" or "life" or "anger" or "pain." "Father" was synonymous with "missing" or "hole." "Father" to me meant "absence of father."

"I don't hate him," I said many times throughout my childhood, my adolescence, and even well into my twenties. I wasn't sure who my father was—the burned photograph, the koala bear, the engagement ring, the tiny cross. "How can you hate someone you don't even know?"

I felt nothing toward him but a cold, almost Zen-like distance. It was rather like facing the impenetrability of a blank sheet of paper right before you started a new story and found the words to mark up the page.

Her Grandfather's Impending Death

The person who came closest to filling the role of surrogate dad was my grandfather—a big, boisterous man with a voice so deep and resonant it could make the hairs on the back of your neck stand on end. He was tall and very handsome in a film-starrish way, and I used to watch, fascinated, as women flirted with him. He was a bartender and manager of a restaurant, and when I was in kindergarten, I would sit and watch the locals drink scotch and bourbon and listen to my grandfather's easy banter. He had a sense of humor that could make even unfunny jokes amusing. He was a very good bartender and a very good grandfather, and the two are not usually inclusive. By the time I met him, he was in his fifties and had apparently settled down a great deal.

Being the last person to emigrate from China in 1938, my grandfather was the only one in the family who spoke with a Chinese accent. He had village tendencies like trapping pigeons under milk crates or catching insects between his fingers. He spoke with a country dialect my grandmother didn't want me to learn, so we got along through half-gestures and phrases that only we understood. Although he had other granddaughters with his last name—whereas mine by Chinese custom indicated that I belonged to some *other* family—the only photograph he kept on his dresser was of me, aged four, in a pink dress with a beribboned front, smiling widely, my front teeth barely grown in.

In the months between meeting my sisters and debating over whether or not to call my father, my grandfather was diagnosed with cancer. It was the first time I had to deal with the impending death of a loved one and it literally changed everything. I started to seriously contemplate the idea of having children. For most of my twenties, I concentrated on my work and career, going through boyfriends after a few years or even a few months. In New York this was considered normal. We were too busy and too broke to be thinking of marriage or children. And it was hard enough finding someone who wanted to be monogamous, much less someone who was willing to get serious and settle down. I still remember getting the key to my then-boyfriend's front door after a solid year of dating, and considering it a huge accomplishment at the time.

My grandfather's diagnosis was a revelation. I was twenty-seven and I wanted to have a family one day. Though I had always assumed that I would be a single mother like my mom, I realized that it was possible to find someone who wanted the same things. Thinking about the future generation made it simple. If I was going to be a good parent, then I needed to find out what happened between my own parents. I needed to answer the biggest question that had eluded me for so many years, and for that, I needed to know who my father was.

Calling Her Father

Making that phone call was the hardest thing I had ever done. I was shaking when I dialed the office number that my sister had given me. It rang a few times before someone picked up. The voice on the other end was shaky and hollow, like wind rattling through an old house. My father was ten years younger than my grandfather, but I was surprised that he sounded much older. After I introduced myself, there was an awkward pause. (As it turned out, his third wife has the same name, and he was struggling to figure out who I was.)

Then I heard the recognition in his voice, followed by the expression of slight irritation over why it had taken me so long to call, which I found annoying (after all, I had been waiting for him my entire life). I wanted to meet soon, while I still had the courage, and was relieved when he agreed to meet a few days later for dinner in Chinatown. He asked if my sisters could join us. I had the sense he wanted to hide behind them if things got too harried with me, so I suggested they meet us later. "I'd like to meet with you alone first."

He agreed smoothly enough, and we confirmed we would meet at his office on Pell Street. For the first time, it would be just the two of us. One on one.

I dreamed two nights later that my father was trying to kill me.

In the dream, I was in a strange, unfamiliar apartment. I couldn't see him, but he was hiding in the shadows with a knife. I woke up terrified and alone, in the middle of the night in my own Brooklyn bedroom. I tried to calm down and listen for any strange noises, but all I could hear was the rush of traffic over the sound of my own breathing.

Meeting Her Father

He was dark-haired and distinguished. He wore a tailored suit and was handsome in that way much older men can be. We met at his office on 3 Pell Street, which I'd passed numerous times before but had never noticed, despite his name on the plaque emblazoned on the wall. His handshake was strong for his lean build, and he seemed tall, though I realized he was, in fact, not much taller than I was as we walked up the stairs to the second floor office.

His office was tiny and spare. There was a front vestibule, where the secretary had once sat, but which now, in my father's semi-retirement, was empty. Covering the walls were black-and-white photographs of him shaking hands with Bobby Kennedy and Donald Manus, the Queens borough president with whom he had shared an office in Jamaica, and who later committed suicide in the 1980s. By his desk were the campaign shots of my father, in his late thirties, taken around the time I was born. His hair was rakishly wavy, and he looked serene and confident in his picture above a row of stars. Along the bookshelves and on his desk, were framed photos of my sisters when they were children—sitting on boats, or at the beach house on the New Jersey shore. There were snapshots of former wives and his stepdaughter. I felt some envy, for this life I never had, but these feelings didn't really come out until later, after I had processed all the new information. I was still struggling with my father as a tangible reality.

We sat and talked for a few minutes, and I searched his face for traces of myself. I had always been told I looked like him, and my sister had said we had the same high forehead. There were similarities, the same red-town eyes with the propensity for dark circles; the same shaped nose, face, and indeed, the same forehead. But, while I was prepared to see physical similarities, I was not expecting to recognize similarities in outward temperament. As he guardedly told me about his life, his run in politics, his wives after my mother, I noticed it. A certain carefulness of speech. A purposefully calm exterior. He had the same way of talking that I did when I was on the extreme defensive. Later, I would see that we even had the same way of walking.

Instead of making me happy, however, these realizations just made me angry. I did not want to admit I had inherited more than just similar looks from this man who had abandoned my mother. Did that mean that I had inherited other tendencies from him too? My mother always said that we sounded alike, especially when I was being "obnoxious," but I always dismissed these claims as being based solely on bitterness. Could my manner and personal demeanor, which I considered entirely my own, be from him? And if so, what other traits had I inherited? A charming but flawed personality? A cavalier attitude and a roving eye? An unwillingness to settle down and take responsibility for my actions?

We left his office a few minutes later to go to dinner. Walking through the crowded narrow streets of old Chinatown, he was very much on the defensive, even as he leaned forward a little, casually pointing out buildings associated with the family. The red brick apartment building where he grew up, on the curved foot of Mott Street. The Chin family Association a few blocks away where my cousin still lived, with its red lettered sign in large Chinese characters over the door. He was making small pleasantries, but didn't ask about me or why I had wanted to meet, fearing an attack. So I purposely asked him questions about his life, centered around the time that I was born, to put him at ease. He rambled on as we crossed Canal Street, speaking more enthusiastically than he parhaps was feeling.

We entered a tiny restaurant, where he knew the owner, and were seated near the front. It was the first time I had heard his side of the story, and as you would expect from Chinatown's number-two lawyer, he spoke very eloquently about his life. Around the time I was born, he was in his late thirties, and his career was in full bloom. There was his thriving practice, which benefited from his being one of the few Chinese-American lawyers in the city. He represented our family's *tong*—which was one of the first family associations in the country and directly involved in New York's bloody *tong* wars of the 1910s and 1920s. There was his club, Nobody's, and the celebrity rock stars who'd hung out there. His political career was promising—the family had clout, and he was popular in the Lower East Side. But when a group of radical leftists split the democratic vote, he lost the election to the incumbent; he was certain he would have won, if not for their interference. (When I asked what platform he had run on, he said without the slightest trace of guilt and in spite of the fact I was sitting right before him, that he "firmly believed in abortion and a woman's right to choose.") He told me about his third wife, Lisa, a sexy stewardess he'd married and divorced twice. They used to compete in international hustle competitions in Hong Kong and China. There was his step-daughter, Sheila, who grew up with my sisters, spending her summers out on the Jersey shore.

He talked at great length throughout dinner. He was quite pleased with the colorfulness of his life, and was reminiscing fondly, when about three-quarters of the way through our meal, I decided to tell him how I felt. I wasn't sure if he could handle it, but I took a deep breath and tried to talk as deliberately and truthfully as possible.

I told him that all he accomplished around 1969 and 1970 was fascinating—the campaign, the club, the different women. My being born at that time, I understood, may have been just one more facet of a period for him that he'd forgotten or quite simply overlooked. I paused for a moment. He was looking at me earnestly from across the table, his hands lowered, the tip of his chopsticks touching his plate. I had what I wanted—his full, undivided attention.

"But for me, that time you weren't there meant everything."

Getting to Know Her Father

We had a short but glorious getting-to-know-you period.

For my twenty-eighth birthday that year, he joined me and about a dozen of my friends, including my best friend Leslie, at a dinner party. The present he gave me was a heavy teak-wood sculpture, made by his father, and wrapped in long white paper. It was an elongated carving of a grandfather with a heavy beard, carrying a long staff in one hand, and shielding a grandchild with the other. It was heavy in my hands and I had barely said thank you before the blur of my own tears clouded my vision.

I was holding something the grandfather I had never known had made, and I couldn't stop crying. The mixed emotions were sharp and intense: sheer happiness and pain, joy and anger, and most of all an overriding feeling of relief. Psychologists call this phenomenon "shrinking," and it occurs when athletes who have been training for years finish a big performance and suddenly burst into tears—you see this sometimes during the Olympics. My friends watched—some understanding, others embarrassed—and, according to Leslie, my father, who was sitting next to me, looked like he too was about to break down.

The irony was not lost on me that I was presented with a gift made by this grandfather I'd been estranged from, by the very person who had caused the estrangement in the first place. I was overjoyed but angry. No one could return that lost history, not even the very person who had taken it away from me. Beyond the sound of my own crying, I could hear the buzz of the restaurant, crowded on a Saturday evening. Everyone around me thought I was sad and upset, especially my father who was looking concerned and hesitantly patting my hand.

Really, I was the happiest I'd been in a long time.

Learning More About Her Father's Personality

I wish I could say that we continued to have a wonderful relationship, that we shared many rich father-daughter experiences together. Throughout the spring and summer of 1998 we were in touch—he bought me a share in my sister's summer house on Fire Island, and I spent some time with him and my sisters. I put the wooden grandfather carving on a special place on my bookshelf and dusted it often. But the next year, his girlfriend from Los Angeles, who was having drug problems, wanted to come to New York so they could be together, and he set her up in a rehab clinic in Manhattan.

My father, I was soon to learn, was like a child who could only focus on what was right in front of him at the moment: a truck, a stuffed animal, a daughter, it didn't matter. Like yesterday's toys we were interchangeable. He could only concentrate on one woman at a time, and when his girlfriend came to town, it meant that he wouldn't return my phone calls or my letters. For my sisters, who went through all of his many marriages and divorces, this was familiar terrain. Kristine, especially, verbally walked me through it.

In the end, my father engaged in a new set of dramas that upset his life *and* theirs: moving in with his girlfriend, catching pneumonia, moving back out when his girlfriend got violent (on withdrawal from crack and cocaine), moving back in when she became clean again. I wish that I could say that he was just having a midlife crisis, that it was a phase he would get over. But my father, who has married and divorced five times during the course of his life, is now seventy years old, and unlikely to change.

Her Mother's Relief

The most remarkable, unexpected outcome of meeting my father was how it affected my relationship with my mother.

We were in the car when I told her about meeting him, on our way to visiting my grandfather. "Do you like him?" she asked, clutching the wheel as we sped through the old neighborhood in Kew Garden Hills, down 150th Street, past all the new construction. When I hesitated, she said, "It's okay, you can say that you do."

She was open to listening to how I felt about him, and his scattered presence in my life. Instead of being angry as I'd feared all those years, she actually seemed relieved. Her hands visibly relaxed on the wheel. Later, she promised to kill him if he hurt me.

As time went by, I noticed the unmistakable change in her. It was as if the air had been let out of a pressurized tank. She was calmer, happier, and somehow more liberated. She seemed more beautiful to me now than I had ever seen her before, even in her twenties and thirties. I realized that her anger had somehow connected her to him, and for all these years it had also held her back. It was only after I had met him that she could finally let go.

We have talked about her resentment over raising me alone, and how her anger toward him sometimes trickled down to me. It was wrong, she finally admitted, to burn his photograph in front of me when I was so young. She was sorry that she had done it. But she was never ashamed of me, as I'd feared for so many years. The shame and bitterness she felt was over being a single mother, not of being *my* mother.

As the years progressed, I kept her informed about my father. His errant ways, and our unsteady relationship. His [escape artist Harry] Houdini "now you see me, now you don't" behavior. How I was slowly coming to accept it all.

It was the same old thing, I told her over the phone a little while ago. We were really better off without him.

Wondering About Inherited Traits

Sometimes, I wonder how it will be for me. If having two parents who were more in love with being in love has indeterminately affected my own chances of weathering marriage. Am I doomed to repeat the patterns of the past? Take away the nurture component of the old "nature vs. nurture" paradigm and consider for a moment the possibilities of genetic determination: Do two fools for love, blindly fumbling around in the dark, beget another fool—as two blond parents are prone to having a blond child? Do two intellectuals bring forth a spate of ivy-leaguers? Do two racists naturally beget a racist, or is it possible for them to produce an ardent liberal? Can two musical illiterates bless the world with a musical genius?

Now in the third year of knowing each other, I still have very mixed feelings about my father. For my mother and her family it is easier: to her, he is the charming and dynamic man who left and broke her heart; for my grandmother, he is the man who ruined her daughter. For me, it is much more complex. I have to contend with the reality that the man who left my mother pregnant to jet-set across the continents with another woman, is in fact, my own father. And that's something I will always have to negotiate, even as I try to deal with the past and toy with the idea of having a family of my own one day.

Part of becoming an adult, I am learning, is shouldering the responsibilities of being a daughter or a son. I keep thinking that I want to honor and respect this, despite the disappointment I feel about my father. I see him now only on rare occasions like Chinese New Year or Father's Day. And even when he forgets simple things, like my birthday or to call to see how I'm doing, I make an effort and phone him when too many months have gone by. Maybe a component of maturing is swallowing the kind of bitterness old Chinese ladies are always talking about. Maybe it means still being a good daughter, even when a parent isn't being a good parent.

I am happy that I met him. The tangible is always preferable to a myth, no matter how dramatic or grandiose. As novelist Mona Simpson wrote in *The Lost Father*, all anyone needs to do to reach god-like status is to walk out. Somewhere along the line, I became tired of mythologizing spare parts, looking for clues in misplaced objects and old photographs. And for the first time, I feel a range of conflicting emotions toward him that alternate between anger, pain, sorrow, and even a hint of tenderness.

Early on when I met my father, I asked him why he had married so many times. His answer was immediate, almost childlike in its logic. "You fall in love. You decide to marry. If it doesn't work out, you get a divorce." He made it sound so simple, like an if-then statement in basic mathematics. But I suspect not even he truly believes this, that you can walk away so unaffected, debt-free.

Organizations to Contact

The editors have compiled the following list of organizations concerned with the issues debated in this book. The descriptions are derived from materials provided by the organizations. All have publications or information available for interested readers. The list was compiled on the date of publication of the present volume; the information provided here may change. Be aware that many organizations take several weeks or longer to respond to inquiries, so allow as much time as possible.

American Bar Association (ABA) Section of Family Law
321 N. Clark St., Chicago, IL 60610
(312) 988-5145 • Fax: (312) 988-6800
e-mail: familylaw@abanet.org
Web site: http://www.abanet.org/family/home.html

The ABA Section of Family Law is an association of lawyers, associates, and law students across the country and worldwide. Members are dedicated to serving the field of family law in areas such as divorce, custody, military law, alternative families, elder law, and children's law. The organization provides resources on divorce in both print and online formats.

American Association for Marriage and Family Therapy (AAMFT)
112 South Alfred St., Alexandria, VA 22314-3061
(703) 838-9808 • Fax: (703) 838-9805
e-mail: central@aamft.org
Web site: http://www.aamft.org/index-nm.asp

The American Association for Marriage and Family Therapy (AAMFT) is the professional association for the field of marriage and family therapy. Marriage and family therapists are professionals who help families and couples work through relationship problems and also mental and emotional disorders. The association facilitates research and education, and develops standards for training, professional ethics, and the clinical practice of marriage and family therapy. The organization publishes a variety of materials that inform the public about the fields of marriage and family therapy.

Association for Children for Enforcement of Support (ACES)
3474 Raymont Blvd. 2nd Floor
University Heights, OH 44118
(800) 738-2237
e-mail: aces@childsupport-aces.org
Web site: www.childsupport-aces.org

ACES is a nonprofit child-support organization dedicated to assisting disadvantaged children whose parents fail to meet the legal and moral obligations of child support and/or visitation. It is the largest national grassroots child-support advocacy organization in the United States, with 40,000 members and 165 chapters in forty-five states.

Association of Family and Conciliation Courts (AFCC)
6525 Grand Teton Plaza, Madison, WI 53719
(608) 664-3750 • Fax: (608) 664-3751
e-mail: afcc@afccnet.org
Website: www.afccnet.org

Founded in 1963, the AFCC has grown from a handful of California counselors and judges to an international association of judges, lawyers, mediators, custody evaluators, parent educators, court administrators, counselors, researchers, academics, and other professionals dedicated to the resolution of family conflict. Members attempt to find creative solutions to divorce-related issues such as child custody mediation, parenting coordination, and divorce education. In addition to annual conferences, the AFCC regularly publishes a journal, *Family Court Review*, as well as books and pamphlets addressing contemporary issues in the family court system.

Child Wefare League of America (CWLA)
2345 Crystal Drive, Suite 250, Arlington, VA 22202
(703) 412-2400 • Fax: (703) 412-2401
Web site:www.cwla.org

Founded in 1920, the CWLA is a membership-based child welfare organization. Its primary objective is to make children a national priority by providing direct support to agencies that serve children and families. In addition to sponsoring annual conferences and providing consultation services to child welfare agencies, the CWLA regularly publishes many different types of materials concerning child welfare issues.

Children's Rights Council (CRC)
6200 Editors Park Drive, Suite 103, Hyattsville, MD 20782
(301) 559-3120
e-mail: info@crckids.org
Web site: http://crckids.org/index.htm

The Children's Rights Council (CRC) is a nonprofit organization that serves divorced, never-married families, extended families, and at-risk youth. CRC promotes a society where laws, attitudes, and public opinion affirm that "The Best Parent is Both Parent." Organized to serve the public purpose of advocating the healthy development of children, it is the mission of CRC to minimize emotional, physical, and economic abuse; the neglect and distress of children; and the development of at-risk behaviors following relationship breakups between parents involved in highly conflicted marital disputes. CRC works to assure a child frequent, meaningful, and continuing contact with two parents and the extended family the child would normally have during a marriage.

Concerned Women for America (CWA)
1015 Fifteenth St. NW, Suite 1100, Washington, DC 20005
(202) 488-7000 • Fax: (301) 559-3124
Web site:www.cwfa.org

The CWA is an educational and legal defense foundation that seeks to strengthen the traditional family by employing Christian principles. In addition to providing a collection of the latest research and news concerning the maintenance of the nuclear family, the CWA publishes *Family Voice*, a monthly magazine for members, and offers many brochures and pamphlets including *Why Children Need Fathers: Five Critical Trends.*

Divorce Care
PO Box 1739, Wake Forest, NC 27588
(800) 489-7778
e-mail: info@divorcecare.org
Web site: www.divorcecare.com

Divorce Care is sponsored by Church Initiative, Inc., a nondenominational, nonprofit ministry, providing thousands of churches in the United States, Canada, the United Kingdom, South Africa, Australia, and several other countries with videos and other media that focus on maintaining strong family bonds. Divorce Care groups meet weekly to support members who are going through divorces. The organization also sponsors Divorce Care for Kids, which helps children deal with their parents' divorce.

Family Research Council (FRC)
801 G St. NW, Washington, DC 20001
(202) 393-2100 • Fax: (202) 393-2134
Web site:www.frc.org

The FRC supports traditional marriage and family using Judeo-Christian values. It has helped shape public debate and formulated public policy that upholds the institutions of marriage and the family. The organization has consistently called for the repeal of no-fault divorce laws in all fifty states. In addition to numerous position papers and research reports, the FRC also publishes two journals, *InFocus* and *Family Policy.*

Kids' Turn
1242 Market Street, 2nd Floor
San Francisco, CA 94102-4802
(415) 437-0700

e-mail: kidsturn@earthlink.net
Web site: www.kidsturn.org

Kids' Turn is a nonprofit organization that helps children understand and cope with the loss, anger, and fear that often accompany separation or divorce. The organization also helps parents understand what support their children need during this crisis in their lives, so that at-risk behavior by children is averted. Kids' Turn is dedicated to enhancing the lives of these children through improved communication and the knowledge they are not alone.

National Association of Child Advocates (NACA)
1522 K St. NW, Suite 600, Washington, DC 20005
(202) 289-0777 • Fax: (202) 289-0776

NACA is a network of state and local child-advocacy organizations addressing important issues such as government allocations for children, child health insurance programs, welfare reform, state legislation affecting kids, and leadership training for child advocates. NACA strives to change policy in areas of health care, education, child care, child support, and juvenile justice. Although NACA and its forty-four member organizations do not provide individual services, they can provide information on the most current legislation and policies affecting children and families.

National Fatherhood Initiative (NFI)
101 Lake Forest Blvd., Suite 360, Gaithersburg, MD 20877
(301) 948-0599 • Fax: (301) 948-4325
Web site: www.fatherhood.org

The NFI is a nonprofit organization that seeks to improve the well-being of children by increasing the proportion of children growing up with involved, responsible, and committed fathers. Through public awareness campaigns and research, the NFI attempts to educate the public about issues facing fathers and their children. Some of the NFI's publications include *Pop's Culture: A National Survey of Dads' Attitudes on Fathering, With This Ring . . . A National Survey of Marriage and the Family,* and *Father Facts.*

National Organization of Single Mothers (NOSM)
PO Box 68, Midland, NC 28107
(704) 888-5437 • Fax: (704) 888-1752
e-mail: info@singlemothers.org
Web site: www.singlemothers.org

NOSM is a nonprofit organization dedicated to helping single mothers cope with the challenges of raising children alone. In addition to providing online support groups, the organization also publishes a quarterly magazine, *Single Mother: A Support Group in Your Hand*, and a resource book, *The Complete Single Mother: Reassuring Answers to Your Most Challenging Concerns*, now in its third edition.

National Stepfamily Resource Center (NSRC)
e-mail: Stepfamily@auburn.edu
Web site: www.stepfamilies.info

The National Stepfamily Resource Center (NSRC) is a division of Auburn University's Center for Children, Youth, and Families (CCYF). In 2006, the Stepfamily Association of America (SAA) voted not to renew its independent organization 501(c)(3) nonprofit status and donated its history, Web site, and experts network to support the development and expansion of The NSRC. Adopting SAAC's vision, the NSRC's primary objective will be serving as a clearinghouse of information, linking family science research on stepfamilies and best practices in work with couples, and children in stepfamilies. The organization publishes *Your Stepfamily Magazine* online, conducts training institutes for family life and marriage educators, therapistst, and counselors, provides consulting on stepfamily issues, and develops educational materials for use with stepfamilies.

Nemours Foundation
252 Chapman Road, Newark, DE 19702
(302) 444-9100 • Fax: (302) 444-9200
e-mail: izenberg@KidsHealth.org
Web site: http://www.kidshealth.org/index.html

Nemours, established in 1936 by philanthropist Alfred I. du-Pont, is dedicated to improving the health and spirit of children. Nemours also creates high-impact educational projects that positively affect the health of children. These projects are developed through the Nemours Center for Children's Health Media, a division of Nemours completely dedicated to this task. The Center creates award-winning, family-friendly health information in a number of formats, including print, video, and online. Their KidsHealth and TeensHealth Web sites include sections on coping with parents' divorce.

North American Conference for Separated & Divorced Catholics (NACSDC)
PO Box 10, Hancock, MI 49930-0010
(906) 482-0494 • Fax: (906) 482-7470
e-mail: office@nasdc.org
Web site: http://www.nacsdc.org/

NACSDC is a Catholic ministry for divorced and separated Catholics, sanctioned by the U.S. Conference of Catholic Bishops and working to create a network of support for families experiencing separation and divorce. NACSDC seeks to improve the entire family's experience of divorce by addressing the religious, emotional, financial, and parenting issues relative to separation, divorce, and remarriage.

Parents Without Partners, Inc.
1650 South Dixie Highway, Suite 510, Boca Raton, FL 33432
(800) 637-7974 • Fax: (561) 395-8557
Web site: http://www.parentswithoutpartners.org/

Parents Without Partners, Inc., is an international, nonprofit membership organization devoted to the welfare and interests of single parents and their children. The organization provides single parents and their children with an opportunity for enhancing personal growth, self-confidence, and sensitivity towards others by offering an environment for support, friendship, and the exchange of parenting techniques.

Sandcastles Program
PO Box 402691, Miami Beach, FL 33140
(205) 978-5000 • Fax: (205) 978-5005
e-mail: mgary@mgaryneuman.com
Web site: www.mgaryneuman.com

The Sandcastles Program is an internationally recognized program designed to help children heal after their parents' divorce. It is a three-and-a-half-hour, onetime group session for children of divorce between the ages of six and seventeen. The program was first instituted in Miami-Dade County, Florida, and is now mandatory there and in over a dozen other jurisdictions throughout the country. In these counties, no final divorce decree will be granted any couple whose minor children do not participate in the Sandcastles Program. M. Gary Neuman, the founder of the Sandcastles Program, is a psychotherapist, a rabbi, and the author of several books, including *Helping Your Kids Cope with Divorce the Sandcastles Way*.

Single Parent Resource Center (SPRC)
31 E. Twenty-eighth St., 2nd Fl., New York, NY 10016
(212) 951-7030
Web site: www.singleparentusa.com

SPRC, an independent nonprofit organization, was founded in 1975 by the Community Service Society of New York to provide services and support for single parents. SPRC sponsors Single Parent USA, an online clearinghouse for information on single-parent organizations in the United States and around the world, to enable single-parent groups and organizations to share information on program development, service models, and techniques and to facilitate referral of single parents to groups or support programs in their local communities.

For Further Research

Books

Constance R. Ahrons, *We're Still Family: What Grown Children Have to Say about Their Parents' Divorce*. New York: HarperCollins, 2004.

Alison Clarke-Stewart and Cornelia Brentano, *Divorce: Causes and Consequences*. New Haven, CT: Yale University Press, 2006.

Mark J. Kittleson, gen. ed., *The Truth about Divorce*. New York: Facts On File, 2005.

Cynthia MacGregor, *The Divorce Helpbook for Teens*. Atascadero, CA: Impact Publishers, 2004.

Elizabeth Price, *Divorce and Teens: When a Family Splits Apart*. Berkeley Heights, NJ: Enslow Publishers, 2004.

Isolina Ricci, *Mom's House, Dad's House for Kids: Feeling at Home in One Home or Two*. New York: Fireside, 2006.

Zoe Stern, Evan Stern, and Ellen Sue Stern, *Divorce Is Not the End of the World: Zoe's and Evan's Coping Guide for Kids*. Berkeley, CA: Tricycle Press, 1997.

Trudi Strain Trueit, *Surviving Divorce: Teens Talk about What Hurts and What Helps*. New York: Scholastic, 2007.

Periodicals

Carolyn M. Brown, "Plotting a New Direction: Arthur Vaughn Is Rebuilding His Finances After Divorce," *Black Enterprise*, September 2004.

Bryan Doerries, "Gio's Journal: Writing about His Feelings Has Helped This Teen Cope with the Breakup of His Parents' Marriage," *Scholastic Choices*, November-December 2006.

Stephen Gandel, "A Divorced Dad Faces Fiscal Reality: As Shared Custody Grows More Common, More and More Men Feel the Financial Pain of Single Parenthood," *Money*, November 1, 2005.

Anne Kingston, "The 27-Year Itch: The Only Age Group in Which Divorce is On the Rise is People over 50. Couples Used to Stick It Out. Not Anymore. Enough is Enough," *Maclean's*, January 29, 2007.

Joanne Malino, "'How I Survived my Parents' Divorce': When Her Family Fell Apart, CG!'S Joanne Malino Learned Her Friends Were the Glue that Could Hold Her Together," *CosmoGirl!* August 2006.

Michael J. McManus, "The Marriage Debate: More Than a Gay Issue," *America*, February 9, 2004.

Sean Price, "Divorce Pains: What Does a 13-Year-Old Girl Have in Common with Two NBA Stars? All Three Have Survived a Breakup between their Respective Parents," *Scholastic Choices*, November–December 2005.

Index

E

F

G

H

I

R

S

T

U

W